Library of
Davidson College

INFORMAL EDUCATION, SELF-CONCEPT, AND READING ACHIEVEMENT: A RESEARCH STUDY

MARY A. PINE

San Francisco, California
1977

428.4
P649i

Published By

R AND E RESEARCH ASSOCIATES
4843 Mission Street, San Francisco 94112
18581 McFarland Avenue, Saratoga, California 95070

Publishers

Robert D. Reed -and- Adam S. Eterovich

Library of Congress Card Catalog Number

77-081028

ISBN

0-88247-483-9

Copyright 1977

By

Mary Anne Pine

81-5010

ACKNOWLEDGEMENTS

The writer wishes to express her sincere appreciation and gratitude to the ten principals for their permission to conduct this study in their schools; to the first grade children and their teachers who cooperated with the writer in providing the necessary data, and to Dr. Louis Aikman for his advice and assistance.

Special appreciation is extended to Dr. Roselmina Indrisano whose expert guidance, interest and caring did much to facilitate the completion of this study.

A big "I love you" is due my husband Jerry and my children David, Maureen and Sean. Without their continued cooperation and support this study would have been only an unfulfilled dream.

TABLE OF CONTENTS

	Page
ACKNOWLEDGEMENTS	iii
LIST OF TABLES	vii
LIST OF ILLUSTRATIONS	ix

Chapter

I. INTRODUCTION 1

    Statement of the Problem 1
    Justification of the Study 1
    Definition of Terms 4
    Purposes of the Study 5
    Research Questions 6

II. REVIEW OF RELATED RESEARCH 9

    Emotions, Personality and Reading Achievement 9

        Causal Relationship 9
        Personality, Emotions and Reading 10
        Emotions and Personality as Predictors of
            Reading Success 13

    Self-Concept and Reading Achievement 14

        Studies which Support the Relationship between
            Self-Concept and Reading Achievement 14
        Studies which Question the Relationship between
            Self-Concept and Reading Achievement 16
        Self-Concept and Reading Readiness 17
        Causal Relationship 17

    The Teacher and Self-Concept 18

    Classroom Organization, Reading Achievement and
        Self-Concept 23

        Individualized Reading and Ability Groups 23
        Individualized Reading and Self-Concept 26
        The Activity-Centered Classroom 26
        Reading Instruction in the Informal Classroom 27
        Reading Achievement in the Informal Classroom 28

    Chapter Summary 30

Chapter		Page
III.	THE DESIGN AND METHODOLOGY OF THE STUDY	42
	Purposes of the Study	42
	Overview of the Design of the Study	43
	Preliminary Considerations	44
	Initiating the Study	45
	Data Collection	46
	Chapter Summary	50
IV.	ANALYSIS OF THE DATA	54
	Description of the Sample	55
	Research Questions	57
	Descriptive Data	67
	Chapter Summary	80
V.	SUMMARY AND IMPLICATIONS FOR FURTHER RESEARCH AND FOR TEACHING	84
	Summary	84
	Conclusions	84
	Limitations of the Study	88
	Implications for Teaching	89
APPENDIX		91
BIBLIOGRAPHY		98

LIST OF TABLES

Table		Page
1.	Mean Chronological Age of Children in the Activity-Centered and Traditional Classrooms, Standard Deviations and F Ratios	55
2.	Distribution of Boys and Girls in the Activity-Centered and Traditional Classrooms	55
3.	Mean IQ Scores of Children in the Activity-Centered and Traditional Classrooms, Standard Deviations and F Ratios	56
4.	Mean Pre Self-Concept Scores of Children in the Activity-Centered and Traditional Classrooms, Standard Deviations and F Ratios	56
5.	Mean Reading Readiness Scores of Children in the Activity-Centered and Traditional Classrooms, Standard Deviations and F Ratios	57
6.	Intercorrelation Matrix of All Variables	58
7.	Correlations Between Pre Self-Concept and Reading Readiness	59
8.	Correlations Between Pre Self-Concept and Reading Achievement	59
9.	Observed and Adjusted Reading Achievement Mean Scores	60
10.	Univariate Analysis of Classroom Organization and Pre Self-Concept on Reading Achievement	60
11.	Correlations Between Reading Achievement and Post Self-Concept	61
12.	Mean Post Self-Concept Scores of Children in the Activity-Centered and Traditional Classrooms, Standard Deviations and F Ratios.	62
13.	Observed and Adjusted Post Self-Concept Mean Scores	63
14.	Univariate Analysis of Classroom Organization and Reading Achievement on Post Self-Concept	63
15.	Mean Reading Achievement Test Scores by Classroom Organization, Reading Readiness and Classroom Organization X Reading Readiness	64
16.	Summary Table - 4 Way Analysis of Variance: Classroom Organization, Reading Readiness and Reading Achievement	64

Table		Page
17.	Mean Reading Achievement Scores by Classroom Organization, Standard Deviations and F Ratios	65
18.	Observed and Adjusted Reading Achievement Mean Scores	66
19.	Univariate Analysis of Classroom Organization and Post Self-Concept on Reading Achievement	66
20.	Pre Adjective Check List Standard Scores and Means	68
21.	Post Adjective Check List Standard Scores and Means	72
22.	Pre and Post Mean Standard Scores on The Adjective Check List	76
23.	Instructional Materials Available	78
24.	Teacher Attitude Toward Materials Available	79

LIST OF ILLUSTRATIONS

Figure		Page
1.	Profile Sheet for The Adjective Check List - Pre Personality Profile	70
2.	Profile Sheet for The Adjective Check List - Post Personality Profile	74

CHAPTER I

INTRODUCTION

For years the teaching of reading has been undertaken in a very structured manner. Emphasis has been on methods, materials, word games, drills, purple dittos, and workbooks. In most instances the overall instructional program of the classroom is determined by the teacher to the degree that the children must adjust themselves to the curriculum and have very few if any opportunities to make choices and focus on their interests. Despite the emphasis placed on the teaching of reading in these classrooms, many children have either failed to accomplish this task or are reading at levels far below their capacity. Perhaps the reason for this lack of achievement is that sufficient thought has not been given to the affective dimensions of the child.

There are those who contend that a change from the traditional classroom organization and its approaches to one which is more child centered would enhance both the cognitive and affective development of the child. The underlying philosophical basis for this assumption is that all human beings have potential and want to learn. However, the type of class room in which the learning occurs is an essential consideration. Recognition must be given to the reciprocal relationship and influence which exist between cognition and affect.

Although there is not a consensus in the findings of investigations which have explored the relationship between self-concept and reading achievement, the research supports the viewpoint that such a relationship does, in fact, exist. Caution must be exercised, however, before one assumes that either the self-concept determines reading achievement or that reading achievement shapes the self-concept. In referring to self-concept and achievement, Purkey writes:

> It may be that the relationship between the two is caused by some factor yet to be determined. The best evidence now available suggests that it is a two-way street, that there is continuous interaction between the self and academic achievement and that each directly influences the other.[1]

It is quite feasible that one of the "factors yet to be determined" is classroom organization. Certainly this is an area of current concern which is worthy of exploration in terms of its effects on self-concept and reading achievement.

Statement of the Problem

This study seeks to investigate and describe the relationship between self-concept, reading readiness and reading achievement of first grade pupils. Further, this study attempts to determine if a relationship exists between the traditional classroom, the activity-centered classroom and reading achievement. Finally this study investigates the interrelationships among classroom organization, self-concept, reading readiness and reading achievement.

Justification of the Study

There are two aspects of self-concept theory about which most psychologists appear to be in agreement:

(1) An individual's self-perceptions include his view of himself as compared to others, his view of how others perceive him, and his view of how he wishes he could be.

(2) An individual's self-perceptions are also largely based upon the experiences which he has had with those people who are significant to him.

A fundamental thesis of this perceptual point of view is that behavior is influenced not only by the accumulation of past and present experiences but also by the personal meanings attached to the perception of those experiences. In other words, behavior is not only a function of what happens to the individual from the outside, it is also a function of how the individual feels on the inside.

That behavior and learning are functions of the self-concept has been adequately demonstrated in the writings of Combs and Snygg, Maslow, Kelley and Rogers.[2] In essence they posit that the adequate person has an essentially positive view of self which has developed not only from many successful experiences but also from an attitude of self-worth and ability to cope. The person of high self-concept looks on life and its challenges as an adventure. If he should experience failure, it is kept in perspective. He recognizes that he has failed in this particular instance; however, he does not feel that he *is* a failure. He continues to see himself as an able human being and confronts each new experience from this vantage point. Because he feels he can cope, he generally does. Thus, he accumulates many successes, the internal reactions to which support and enhance his already positive self-concept.

On the other hand, people who are relatively inadequate tend to view themselves quite negatively. Lacking a feeling of self-worth, they tend to perceive themselves as unliked, unwanted and unable to cope with problems. The tendency to focus on their inadequacies causes them to lose touch with their strengths and abilities. When situations are encountered they expect not only to encounter insurmountable difficulties but also to fail. Again the self-fulfilling prophecy is completed. One failure brings about others with accompanying feelings of inadequacy, helplessness and inferiority. The on-going result being a further lowering of self-concept.

Psychologists and educators are becoming far more aware of the fact that how a person views himself is closely connected to how he behaves and learns.[3] Why is it that some children with high IQ scores do not receive correspondingly high academic grades? Have they learned to see themselves as incapable? On the other hand, why is it that some children with average intelligence test scores perform with remarkable success in the academic world? Is it that they see themselves as able, coping individuals and therefore perform accordingly? "Research is teaching us that how a student (or anyone else for that matter) performs depends not only on how intelligent he actually is, but how intelligent he thinks he is."[4]

As the child enters school, the major task which confronts him is that of learning to read. American society places a high value on this skill and as a result the child senses that both his parents and teachers consider this accomplishment vital. This is the first major academic situation with which he must cope and which adds a significant dimension to his definition of self. How will he function? Will his self-concept affect his success in handling this challenge? Will his self-concept be affected by his success or failure in accomplishing this task? Knowledge of the relationship between self-concept and human behavior and learning, indicates that the child who brings a positive self-concept to the task of learning to read will meet with greater success than the child who has a negative self-concept. It can also be expected that a low reading score will have a negative effect on the child's self-concept and that a high reading score will have a positive effect on the child's self-concept.

It is hypothesized that reading competence and self-concept will be enhanced in an activity-centered classroom in which the following are characteristic:

(1) instruction is carefully personalized in an attempt to meet the individual needs, interests and abilities of children, thus providing maximum opportunity for success and lessening the possibilities of threat to the ego.

(2) the materials provided are perceived as meaningful and relevant to the child.

(3) there is freedom to pursue personal interests, raise questions, make decisions, explore and discover.

(4) provocative interest centers and materials of the type which demand pupil interaction and constant investigation are provided in an attempt to bring about self-initiated learning.

(5) an attitude of competitiveness need not exist as each child is appreciative of the value of his own personal growth and development.

(6) the child has the freedom to make mistakes and still feel competent.

(7) opportunities are provided for the child to grow socially, emotionally and intellectually, through working as an individual, as well as in a wide variety of group and peer learning situations.

(8) respect, trust, love and concern for one another are nurtured.

(9) emphasis is placed on both the affective and cognitive development of the child.

(10) the teacher's role is one of facilitator of learning rather than a disseminator of information.

If this type of classroom were provided for children, would their self-concepts be enhanced? Would this increase in self-concept help each child to see himself as an achiever in reading? Would this feeling of effectiveness be reflected in increased reading achievement? On the other hand, would the comparative lack of structure of the activity-centered classroom produce a decline in self-concept? Would this decrease in self-concept cause the child to perceive himself as ineffective in reading? Would this feeling of ineffectiveness be reflected in low reading achievement? Or would this investigation indicate that the traditional classroom environment, with its conventional approach to the teaching of reading, does in fact enhance the development of self-concept and produce better reading achievement?

For over forty years critics of informal education both in England and the United States have charged that this approach to education hinders achievement.[5] Conversely, critics of traditional approaches to education are equally as forceful in purporting that the children not only achieve as well in this type of classroom but that they also have many opportunities to develop as full human beings.

It is essential that evaluations of the cognitive and affective growth of young children in the activity-centered classroom be made. At the present time this researcher has discovered no empirical data to test the assumptions of activity-centered education as these bear on reading achievement and self-concept. It would seem imperative that educators move from speculation about informal education to a more rigorous testing of its effects on the cognitive and affective development of children vis-a-vis the traditional approaches to education. This study will address some aspects of the issues of experimental investigation by focusing on the relationship among self-concept, reading achievement and activity-centered learning.

Definition of Terms

Self-Concept - the scores achieved by the children on The Thomas Self-Concept Values Test,[6] 1969 Edition, which measures the way the child sees himself and the way he believes his mother, teacher and peers see him.

    (a) low self-concept - scores below the fiftieth percentile

    (b) high self-concept - scores at or above the fiftieth percentile

Classroom Organization

    (a) Traditional Classroom - classroom in which the curriculum and the instructional program are determined and prescribed by the teacher to the degree that the children must adjust themselves to the curriculum and program. This classroom is more curriculum oriented than child-centered.

    (b) Activity-Centered Classroom - classroom in which instruction is carefully geared to meet the individual needs and abilities of children; in which play is perceived as a valuable learning experience; which is more child and project centered than teacher dominated; in which the child has the freedom to pursue his own interests, make decisions, explore and discover within the parameters of a curriculum designed to meet his needs. This classroom is frequently referred to as informal and is modeled after the British Infant Schools.

While both of these definitions refer to a specific organizational approach, it must be recognized that the teacher is the most significant variable in the teaching-learning process and that she will bring her personal philosophy of education to whichever organizational pattern she employs.

Reading Achievement - scores achieved by the children on the reading subtests of the Metropolitan Achievement Test.[7]

    (a) low reading achievement - scores below the fiftieth percantile

    (b) high reading achievement - scores at or above the fiftieth percentile

Reading Readiness - scores achieved by the children on the Murphy-Durrell Reading Readiness Analysis.[8]

    (a) low reading readiness - scores below the fiftieth percentile

    (b) high reading readiness - scores at or above the fiftieth percentile

Intelligence - the intelligence quotients yielded by the Pintner-Cunningham Primary Test.[9]

Top Half - in all testing situations, this term refers to the scores of all the children in the study which fell at or above the fiftieth percentile of the scores obtained by the children in both the activity-centered and traditional classrooms.

Bottom Half - in all testing situations, this term refers to the scores of all the children included in the study which fell below the fiftieth percentile of the scores yielded by the children in both the activity-centered and traditional classrooms.

Significant - in the analysis of variance and the analysis of covariance tests of hypotheses, significant refers to statistically significant. Probabilities of .05, .02, .01 and .001 are regarded as statistically significant - i.e., not due to chance.

Significant Correlation - for purposes of this study Garrett's Table for the "Meaning of a coefficient of Correlation" was used. This table is presented as follows:

    r from .00 to $\pm$ .20   very low or negligible
    r from $\pm$ .20 to $\pm$ .40   low; present but slight
    r from $\pm$ .40 to $\pm$ .70   substantial or marked
    r from $\pm$ .70 to $\pm$ 1.00   high to very high[10]

Demonstrated Successful Performance in the Classroom - based on the judgment of the school principal and the reading consultant. A copy of the informal instrument used appears in the Appendix, pp. 91.

Conventional Teacher Preparation - preparation which is primarily campus based with a student teaching component. One in which there are discrete courses with an emphasis on methodology.

Purposes of the Study

The purposes of the study are as follows:

1. To investigate and describe the relationship between pre self-concept and reading readiness.

2. To investigate and describe the relationship between pre self-concept and reading achievement.

    2a. To investigate and describe the interaction effect of pre self-concept and classroom organization on reading achievement:

3. To investigate and describe the relationship between reading achievement and post self-concept.

4. To investigate and describe the difference between the post self-concept scores of children in the activity-centered classrooms and the post self-concept scores of children in the traditional classrooms.

   4a. To investigate and describe the differences between the post self-concept scores of children with high reading achievement scores and the post self-concept scores of children with low reading achievement scores.

   4b. To investigate and describe the interaction effect of classroom organization and reading achievement on post self-concept.

5. To investigate and describe the interaction effect of classroom organization and reading readiness on reading achievement.

   5a. To investigate and describe the differences between the reading achievement scores of children in the activity-centered classrooms and the reading achievement scores of children in the traditional classrooms.

   5b. To investigate and describe the differences between the reading achievement scores of those children who have high post self-concept scores and the reading achievement scores of those children who have low post self-concept scores.

   5c. To investigate and describe the interaction effect of classroom organization and post self-concept on reading achievement.

Research Questions

Consistent with the purposes cited above this study seeks to answer the following questions:

1. What is the relationship between pre self-concept and reading readiness?

2. What is the relationship between pre self-concept and reading achievement?

   2a. What is the interaction effect on pre self-concept and classroom organization on reading achievement?

3. What is the relationship between reading achievement and post self-concept?

4. Will there be a difference between the post self-concept scores of children in the activity-centered classrooms and the post self-concept scores of children in the traditional classrooms?

   4a. Will there be a difference between the post self-concept scores of children with high reading achievement scores and the post self-concept scores of children with low reading achievement scores?

   4b. What is the interaction effect of classroom organization and reading achievement on post self-concept?

5. What is the interaction effect of classroom organization and reading readiness on reading achievement?

   5a. Will there be a difference between the reading achievement scores of children in the activity-centered classrooms and the reading achievement scores of children in the traditional classrooms?

   5b. Will there be a difference between the reading achievement scores of those children who have high post self-concept scores and the reading achievement scores of those children who have low post self-concept scores?

   5c. What is the interaction effect of classroom organization and post self-concept on reading achievement?

Overview of the Design of the Study

Twelve first grade classrooms located in eight communities in the states of New Hampshire and Maine were selected for this study. Six of these classrooms were organized according to traditional patterns, while the remaining six classrooms were activity-centered.

The total sample of two-hundred fifty-seven pupils was administered:

1. a group reading readiness test

2. an individual self-concept test which measures the way the child sees himself, as well as the way he believes his mother, teacher and peers see him.

3. a group intelligence test

4. the reading subtests of a standardized achievement test

5. a post-test administration of the self-concept instrument

In addition, two informal observational visits and three formal observational visits were made by the investigator in each classroom. Teachers completed a personality assessment inventory as well as an inventory of the types of materials which were either in their classroom or available to them in the school for purposes of reading instruction.

The nature, purpose and direction of a research endeavor is to a great extent contingent upon the results of previous research in the field and in related areas. From previous research evolves the problem, the theoretical framework, the formulation of hypotheses and the methods of research appropriate to the solution of the problem. Chapter II presents a review of this research.

Footnotes:

1. William W. Purkey, *Self-Concept and School Achievement* (Englewood Cliffs, New Jersey: Prentice-Hall., 1970), p. 23.

2. Arthur W. Combs and Donald Snygg, *Individual Behavior: A Perceptual Point of View* (New York: Harper and Brothers, 1959); Abraham Maslow, *Motivation and Personality* (New York: Harper and Brothers, 1959); Earl C. Kelley, *Education for What is Real* (New York: Harper and Brothers, 1951); and Carl R. Rogers, Client-Centered Therapy: *Its Current Practice, Implications and Theory* (Boston: Houghton Mifflin Company, 1951).

3. Don E. Hamachek, *Encounters with the Self* (New York: Holt, Rinehart and Winston, Inc., 1971), p. 174.

4. Ibid.

5. Charles E. Silberman, *Crisis in the Classroom* (New York: Random House, 1970), p. 258.

6. Walter L. Thomas, *The Thomas Self-Concept Values Test*, rev. ed. (Grand Rapids, Michigan: Educational Service Company, 1969).

7. Walter N. Durost et al., *Metropolitan Achievement Tests*, rev. ed., Primary 1, Form F (New York: Harcourt Brace Javonovich, Inc., 1970).

8. Helen A. Murphy and Donald D. Durrell, *Murphy-Durrell Reading Readiness Analysis* (New York: Harcourt, Brace & World, Inc., 1965).

9. Rudolph Pintner, Bess V. Cunningham and Walter N. Durost, *Pintner-Cunningham Primary Test*, rev. ed., Form A (New York: Harcourt, Brace & World, Inc. 1964).

10. Henry E. Garrett, *Elementary Statistics* (New York: Longmans, Green and Company, 1956), p. 116.

CHAPTER II

REVIEW OF RELATED RESEARCH

Reports of research studies which have investigated the relationship between emotions, personality and reading achievement have grown in number since the 1920's. Although these investigations have not produced conclusive findings, they may have fulfilled a more worthwhile purpose in prompting current researchers to look more closely at the relationship between self-concept and reading achievement.

The trend toward more innovative approaches in classroom organization coupled with a realization of the impact of the teacher's attitude and behavior on both self-concept and reading achievement, has important implications for those who are interested in the relationship between self-concept and reading. Although research in these latter areas appears to be quite sparse, it does provide an empirical perspective in which to develop a framework for a consideration and analysis of the questions in the present study. These questions have evolved from theoretical investigations of self-concept, reading achievement and activity-centered education.

This chapter reviews the research findings in selected areas of the psychology of reading and achievement as well as the research concerned with the effects of classroom organization on reading achievement. These areas of research are elaborated upon as follows: 1) the relationship between emotions, personality and reading achievement; 2) the relationship between self-concept and reading achievement; 3) teacher-student congruency in appraising the child's self-concept; and 4) the effects of teacher behavior, and teacher attitude on reading achievement. The chapter continues with a presentation of studies which investigated the effect of grouping and individualized reading instruction on self-concept and reading achievement. Finally research on the relationship between the activity-centered classroom and reading achievement is considered.

Emotions, Personality and Reading Achievement

Causal Relationship

The nature of the relationship between emotions and reading has been a topic of interest for many decades. Particular interest has focused on the question of personality. Whether reading problems are the cause of emotional problems or whether emotional problems are the cause of reading problems is a question which continues to intrigue researchers. Numerous investigations have been conducted to determine: 1) if a relationship exists between emotions and reading achievement; 2) whether emotional disturbances do, in fact, underlie reading failure; and 3) if reading problems cause emotional maladjustment.

Unfortunately for those who demand specific answers to these queries, the results of this massive body of research have produced conflicting and ambiguous findings, particularly in the area of causation. In fact, some of the earlier researchers exhibited a tendency to vacillate in formulating conclusions concerning this question.

In 1928, Monroe, after careful study of 175 retarded readers, concluded that while negativism or other unfavorable attitudes may interfere with learning to read, emotional problems probably develop more frequently as a result of failure in reading.[11] Reports of her later work (1935) indicated similar findings.[12] However, in 1937, she supported the hypothesis that many primary emotional factors are causes of reading difficulty.[13]

In referring to emotions and reading, Blanchard wrote, "...the basis of the difficulty may be found, in many instances, in the emotional experience of the child during his first attempts to learn to read.[14] Later, in reporting findings on seventy-three cases who had been seen at the Philadelphia Child Guidance Clinic from 1925 to 1932 she wrote:

> While we do not claim that trouble with reading is invariably of this (emotional) origin, our experience does lead us to believe that it is related to difficulties in emotional development more frequently than has hitherto been realized.[15]

Blancard reverted to her original conclusion in 1946 when she indicated that reading failure and problem behavior are related to the extent that emotional instability may cause reading failure.[16]

The question of causation continued to intrigue researchers for the next two decades. As a result, the literature abounds with reports of clinical studies, case studies, and experimental research which attempted to provide an answer to this question. While the data were equally impressive in regard to reading failure as a cause of emotional disturbance and emotional disturbance as a cause of reading disability, noted authorities concurred that a theory of causation was impractical and impossible to substantiate.

In 1941 Gates wrote:

> All of these symptoms or forms of nervousness, withdrawal, aggression, defeatism, chronic worry appear among cases in which the maladjustment is the cause, the result or the concomitant of reading difficulty. It is therefore not possible to tell whether they were causes or effects or an accompaniment of trouble with reading.[17]

This thinking was substantiated by Russell who in 1948, after reviewing the available evidence, concluded that: "Symptoms such as nervousness, withdrawal, aggression or chronic worry may appear when maladjustment is the cause, the concomitant, or the result of reading disability."[18]

Reaffirmation of this point was made by Smith in 1955 when she stated:

> Research consequently reveals that there is a high incidence of emotional disturbances among children retarded in reading; and that emotional disturbances may cause reading disabilities, or vice versa, both usually being the result of a constellation of causes.[19]

Personality, Emotions and Reading

More recent researchers have investigated the personality characteristics of children who are experiencing difficulty in reading. Of the related studies summarized below three were reported in the 50's, twelve in the 60's and one in the 70's.

Abrams administered two different personality scales to 25 male remedial readers between the ages of 8 and 12 and compared their scores with a matched group of boys who were reading at or above grade level. The findings of this study indicated that there are personality characteristics which differentiate the non-reader from the achieving reader. Abrams concluded that non-readers' feelings of anxiety negatively influence their ability to function efficiently in learning situations that stress attention, concentration and recall. This group of children was also found to be more impulsive, insecure, irritable and less well-adjusted both at home and school than the group of achieving readers.[20]

In subsequent investigations during that decade, Tabarlett found after administering the California Test of Personality to 72 children that, "...poor mental health and reading retardation go together"[21] and Norman and Daley, using the same measure of personality with a group of 42 superior readers and 41 inferior readers, in the sixth grades in 14 middle-class schools of Albuquerque, New Mexico, determined that, "Superior readers achieved significantly higher adjustment scores."[22]

Adjustment factors were also a major focus in a study undertaken by Powell and Bergen in 1962, who examined a variety of behavioral factors related to the performance of 50 conforming and 50 nonconforming male students in grades 10, 11 and 12. Data for the study were obtained on the California Reading Test, the California Test of Personality, the Thurstone Temperament Schedule and a questionnaire designed by the authors to explore home and family conditions, attitudes and friendship patterns. Differences were found favoring the conforming boys at the .05 level of significance or better in reading performance, in school grades, and in fewer examples of absence and tardiness in school.[23]

In 1964 however, Chronister found a positive but only slight relationship between personality factors and reading comprehension,[24] while Durr and Schmatz found no significant differences between gifted overachievers and underachievers as measured by the California Test of Personality.[25]

The purpose of the research undertaken by Zimmerman and Allebrand was to investigate the personality characteristics and attitudes toward achievement of two groups of school children who were differentiated in reading ability. Prior to undertaking this investigation, the researchers hypothesized that poor readers (subjects reading at least two years below grade level) would show less adequate personal adjustment and less productive attitudes toward achievement. A comparison of the results of the scores of 71 poor readers and 82 good readers on the California Test of Personality and card 1 of the Thematic Apperception Test revealed significant differences in personality function. The major discrepancy between the two groups appeared to be more in the area of personal rather than social adjustment specifically, personal worth, withdrawal tendencies, sense of personal freedom, self-reliance, nervous symptoms and feelings of belonging rise. The investigators concluded that poor readers so lacked feelings of personal worth and adequacy that they avoided achievement.[26]

The personality patterns of 28 boys and 12 girls between the ages of 8 and 11 who were reading at a level two years below their mental age were surveyed by Frost. Instruments used in this study were the Porter-Cattell Children's Personality Questionnaire and Scott Bristol Social Guide. Results of this investigation indicated that the sample studied differed from the standardization sample in intelligence, drive and adjustment.[27]

Singer and Pitman, in a study based upon Sullivan's description of hysterical individuals, hypothesized that disabled readers manifested behaviors that were similar to those of hysterics. They reasoned that if the dishonesty, exploitiveness, insincerity and hypocrisy displayed by hysterics is learned from significant others, then hysterics must be acutely cognizant of such behaviors when they are encountered in others; conversely persons free from such symptoms should be less attentive to this bizarre behavior. To test their hypothesis, the responses of 20 seventh grade disabled readers to a modification of the Verbal Absurdities and the Proverb items from the Stanford-Binet were compared to the responses of 20 matched controls with no reading difficulty. Analysis of responses to these items indicated that the underachievers scored higher on the Verbal Absurdities items. The researchers interpreted this result to mean that poor readers were more sensitive to hypocrisy, insincerity and falsehood.[28]

In a similar vein, Schroeder hypothesizing that emotionally disturbed children were retarded in school achievement, attempted to determine whether children classified by their teachers as psychosomatic, aggressive, school phobic, neurotic-psychotic, or school problems exhibited differences in the areas of reading and arithmetic. Using the Jastak Wide Range Achievement Test, the investigator found the mean reading score of the children was consistently lower than the mean arithmetic score.[29]

Athey[30] examined the relationship of reading to personality in terms of dimensions hypothesized from an integration of Holmes' theory of the role of value systems in achievement and Erickson's theory of personality development. To accomplish this task, she administered the Paragraph Meaning subtest of the Stanford Achievement Battery and the University of California Inventory, a personality assessment instrument, to two samples (N = 160 and 130) of ninth grade students. New personality scores were secured by rescoring each test using only the differentiating items. Only seventy items survived double cross-validation at the 5 percent level. Seven factors were then extracted and named as being most differential. These included dependence-docility, negative self-concept, school dislikes, family orientation, anxieties and social relationships. Further analysis of the data indicated that:

> Poor readers were psychologically immature, manifesting a dependency and submissiveness associated with parental treatment. They manifested negative self-concepts about their competence in school work and in social areas such as leadership and popularity. Good readers demonstrated autonomy in school and home. They were more intellectually oriented, liking school and wishing to continue their studies.[31]

Confirmation of the researcher's hypothesis supported the premise that the integrated Holmes-Erickson theory provides a useful framework for understanding the personality dynamics involved in reading.[32]

The personality and behavioral characteristics of good, poor and average readers of first and fourth grades were surveyed by Holzinger in 1967. The sample consisted of 85 first grade and 93 fourth grade boys from six first and six fourth grade classrooms in a midwestern suburb. Each student was measured on five variables of personality and behavioral characteristics. Significant differences were found on nearly all the personality and behavioral characteristics favoring the good readers over the average readers and the average over the poor. An interesting finding of this study was that first grade poor readers scored significantly lower than the good readers on only two variables, those of peer and teacher perception. However, fourth grade poor readers scored significantly lower on all five of the variables; personal adjustment, social adjustment, peer acceptance, peer rejection and pupil behavior.[33]

Stavrianos and Landsman published a report of clinical data on 311 boys aged 6 through 12 who exhibited specific lag in some aspect of the perceptual-motor process. The results of a battery of visual, auditory, laterality, psychological, apitude and achievement tests administered to the subjects who were grouped according to reading status, presence or absence of perceptual-motor dysfunction, IQ and age indicated that few poor readers have normally balanced and mature personalities.[34]

Two studies which suggest that there is not a relationship between emotions and reading achievement were reported during this period. In 1966, Savage investigated the possible relationships between extraversion, neuroticism, intellectual level and school achievement of 93 junior high school boys in England. Scores derived from the <u>Otis Quick Scoring Mental Ability Test</u>, the <u>Eysenk Personality Inventory</u>, the <u>Schonell Essential Mechanical Arithmetic Tests</u> and the <u>Watts Sentence-Reading Tests</u> were intercorrelated in this study. Results indicated that there was a significant relationship between extraversion and IQ and between arithmetic scores and extraversion. Neuroticism was found to be significantly related to reading achievement in a negative direction, however it was not significantly related to either intelligence or arithmetic.[35]

Shapiro, who hypothesized that high reading achievement would be related to high neuoticism and that low reading achievement would be related to high extraversion, used the Vocabulary and Reading Comprehension subtests of the <u>Iowa Test of Basic Skills</u>, the <u>California Test of Mental Maturity</u> as well as the <u>Junior Maudsley Personality Inventory</u> with 50 fifty grade boys, half of whom were high achievers and the other half of whom were low achievers. His data indicated that there was no significant relationship between reading achievement and either personality factor.[36]

Conversely, Bell, Anderson and Lewis reported the findings of a study conducted during this period of time which suggests that low reading achievement causes emotional problems. In this investigation, the researchers studied 50 junior high school black males and 50 white males of the same grade level. In each group of 50, 25 of the students were classified as adequate readers--reading either 6 months above or below the level expected for a student of that chronological age--and 25 were considered inadequate readers--performance 2 or more years below the level expected for a student of that chronological age. Their findings indicate that there was a total of five factors which related to reading deficit. These included: verbal deficits, low socio-economic background, aggression, passivity and negativism. The researchers claimed, based on their data, that the three personality factors were adopted by the low achievers as adjustive patterns of behavior.[37]

Emotions and Personality as Predictors of Reading Success

The possibility that emotional factors may be predictive of low reading achievement was investigated by Ames and Walker in 1964 and by Kagan in 1965. In the former study the researchers compared 54 primary school children's performance on reading tests administered in the fifth grade with their kindergarten scores on the Rorschach and intelligence tests to examine the validity of using the Rorschach to predict later reading ability as well as to determine whether the possible predictive value of the Rorschach was dependent upon intelligence.

The investigators found that individual characteristics do indeed contribute to individual differences in reading. Moreover, they also found that certain items on the Rorschach are likely to be associated with slower progress in reading.[38]

In the second study Kagan endeavored to determine whether measures of reflection-impulsivity collected in first grade would be prognostic of reading achievement one year later. Measures of reading ability, visual analysis and reflection-impulsivity were administered to a group of 130 children in the second half of grade one. Approximately 100 of this group were retested for word recognition early in grade two and again for oral reading and visual analysis at the end of that same year in school. Children, classified as impulsive on the initial testing made more word recognition errors than did the reflective subjects. The results of impulsivity as indicated on designed matching tests collected in grade one were also positively correlated with reading errors in grade two. Kagan's data also showed that fast time response was the better predictor for boys and high error score was the better predictor for girls.[39]

In summary, research on the relationship between emotions, personality and reading achievement generally suggests that there is a relationship between these factors. However, the question of causality remains unanswered. Next, this chapter will consider the nature of the relationship between self-concept and reading achievement.

Self-Concept and Reading Achievement

Although research in the area of personality, emotions and reading is still being conducted, one notes a shift in the research beginning in the early 1960's to an emphasis on self-concept and reading. The following considerations are suggested as explanations of this trend:

1) increased writing and research on the phenomenon of the self-concept as exhibited in the works of such psychologists as Maslow, Rogers, Hamachek, Combs and Snygg.[40]

2) a growing recognition of the fact that emotions and personality are merely manifestations of the self-concept.

3) a resultant appreciation of the fact that more emphasis should be placed on the child in the reading process.

Studies which Support the Relationship between Self-Concept and Reading Achievement

After an investigation of 926 students in grades 4, 5 and 8 Hallock in a factorial design which included sex, intelligence, reading achievement and personality variables found self-reliance and a feeling of personal worth to be among the measures most significantly related to reading achievement.[41]

Bodwin studied the relationships between self-concept and certain disabilities of children in grades 3 through 6. He investigated 100 pupils with reading disabilities, 100 with arithmetic disabilities, and 100 with no educational disabilities and found a significant relationship between immature self-concept and reading disability citing correlations of .72 at the third grade level and .62 at the sixth grade level.[42] Lumpkin not only found a significant relationship between self-concept and reading achievement but also stated, "...with this particular group (underachievers) the self-concept which the individual has influences his behavior in academic work as well as his social relationships.[43]

In an investigation of 361 sixth grade boys, Spicola found that boys who perceived themselves as very low or high in mental ability had reading performances that corresponded to their perceptions of their ability;[44] while Bricklin concluded two years later that among eighth grade boys, a group with comprehension and word recognition problems had more negative self-concepts than either an achieving group or a group with comprehension problems alone.[45]

After evaluating the personality adjustment of fifteen underachieving eighth and ninth grade pupils, as indicated by their performance on the Rorschach, the Thematic Apperception Test and the Mental Health Analyses, Blackman determined that underachievers had significantly poorer mental health than overachievers. Specific differences were found in behavior, emotional stability and concern about physical defects.[46] Similar results were reported two years later by Schwyhart who also explored the relationship of the self-concepts of ninth grade boys who were retarded in reading. In commenting on the findings he states: "For the majority of subjects the answer to the question, 'Do severely retarded readers have characteristically negative patterns of self-concept,' is answered in the affirmative."[47]

After administering the Temple University Reading Clinic Informal Reading Inventory and the Wechsler Intelligence Scale for Children to a large number of children between the ages of 8 and 13, Toller selected for study 50 children of average or above average intelligence, 25 of whom were achieving readers and 25 of whom were underachieving readers. The results of the administration of two author-constructed self-evaluation instruments to the members of each group indicated that there were significant differences between the two groups at the .001 level in self-evaluations. These differences which favored the achievers were in the areas of acceptance, adequacy, as well as personal self and social self-concept.[48]

Williams and Cole investigated, among other factors, the relationship between 80 sixth-graders' scores on the Tennessee Self-Concept Scale and their scores on the reading subtests of the California Achievement Test Battery. Once again a significant positive correlation was obtained between the reading and self-concept scores.[49]

One year later, these findings were upheld by Paddleford's investigation of 238 students in a suburban elementary school. In addition Paddleford's data indicated that a significant positive correlation does not exist between gains in reading achievement and gains in self-concept scores.[50]

Although this latter finding substantiates those of Lovinger's earlier work with kindergarten and first grade children,[51] it refutes the results of Carlton's investigation. In this instance, Carlton found a significant relationship between self-concept development and increased reading achievement, when self-directed dramatization was used with remedial readers.[52]

In the more recent research, the conclusion that there is a relationship between self-concept and reading achievement was also drawn by: Hake, as a result of his investigation of 80 sixth grade students;[53] Cummings, after a study of a carefully selected group of 48 third graders;[54] and by Swartz, who also explored the possibility of this relationship with a group of third grade children.[55]

Studies which Question the Relationship between Self-Concept and Reading Achievement

The studies of Wood and Glick only partially support the hypothesis that self-concept and reading achievement are related. In the latter study Glick, who investigated among other factors the relationship between early school failure and subsequent changes in general and academic self-concepts concluded that although good male readers were more likely to have favorable rather than unfavorable changes in both general and academic self-concept, poor male readers did not score significantly lower as compared to good male readers on either of the self-concept measures employed. Moreover no significant differences were noted for girls.[56] Conversely, Wood in analyzing 585 fifth graders found that boys with higher reading comprehension had higher self-concepts than did boys with average or lower reading comprehension scores. However, there was not a similar finding for girls. In addition Wood's findings indicate that neither boys nor girls who scored higher in word meanings had higher self-concepts than those who scored average or below.[57]

In an early investigation, Carter failed to find any significant differences in achievement between seven year old children who were rated high, medium or low on personal, social and total adjustment.[58]

Later in 1964, Nicholson studied 47 nine year old boys who attended fourth grade in a New York City public school. Upon analysis of the results of test scores obtained on the Rorschach and the Davidson List of Trait Names, he found no significant correlation between measures of self-concept and reading achievement as determined by scores obtained on the reading sub-tests of the <u>Stanford Achievement Test</u>.[59]

More recent investigations were undertaken by Sedarat and Ruhly. In the former study, Sedarat selected subjects from all of the fifth and sixth grades in Janesville, Wisconsin. A group of intellectually superior pupils of both sexes with IQs of 120 or better was selected. Scores from the reading sub-test of the <u>Stanford Achievement Test</u> were then used to select achieving and underachieving readers. From this pool 20 intellectually superior achievers and 20 intellectually superior underachievers were selected on a random basis. Analysis of the scores of each child on two personality measures prompted the conclusion that there was no identifiable relationship between ego strength and reading achievement.[60]

Ruhly explored the relationship of reading achievement to the socio-economic background, reported self-concept and psycholinguistic abilities of 128 second grade children, 64 of whom were considered able readers and 64 of whom were classified as poor readers. Although she found that there was a significant difference between the psycholinguistic abilities of the able and poor readers, she failed to find a significant difference between these two groups in terms of self-adequacy and total self-concept.[61] These findings were substantiated by Lewis in 1972. As a result of her work with 47 first grade children, 22 of whom were simultaneously provided with a program in self-concept development, she found that the treatment group made no significant gains in either self-concept development or reading achievement.[62]

Self-Concept and Reading Readiness

The question of the relationship between self-concept and reading readiness was researched by Giuliani in 1968. Subjects in his study were 366 kindergarten children enrolled in sixteen classrooms of a suburban New York Public School District. When scores obtained on the Metropolitan Reading Readiness Test were compared to those obtained on a self-concept inventory, the investigator concluded that there was a significant positive relationship between reading readiness and self-concept. Giuliani also noted that as self-concept increased reading readiness increased directly.[63]

Causal Relationship

Two studies suggest the possibility of a cause effect relationship between self-concept and reading achievement. Lamy investigated the relationship between kindergarten children's self-perceptions and their world prior to reading instruction and their subsequent achievement in first grade. She found that self-perception scores correlated as highly with reading achievement as did intelligence test scores. Together both scores were found to be better predictors of reading success than either score taken separately. In citing her conclusions, Lamy suggested that the perceptions of the child about himself and his world may be causal factors in his future reading achievement.[64]

Wattenberg and Clifford conducted an exploratory study to determine whether self-concept or reading disability was the antecedent phenomenon. Measures of kindergarten children's self-concepts were obtained through the utilization of self-referent statements obtained as they drew pictures of their family and as they responded to incomplete sentences. These scores were then related to achievement during the second grade. The results showed that: 1) in general, measures of self-concept and ratings of ego strength made at the beginning of kindergarten proved to be somewhat more predictive of reading achievement two and one-half years later than was the measure of mental ability and 2) the self-concept stands in a causal relationship to reading achievement.[65]

The results of these two studies were not supported by Williams, however, who hypothesized that self-concept scores of children were positively correlated with reading achievement in the first and second grade, and that self-concept scores add to the prediction of reading achievement scores beyond intelligence and reading readiness scores. For two successive years, Williams drew subjects from three first grade classrooms and administered an adaptation of the Coopersmith Self-Esteem Inventory and the Metropolitan Reading Readiness Test. At the end of both first and second grade, she also administered the California Achievement Test to these children. Results of a step-wise multiple regression revealed that self-concept failed to add to predictability of either first or second grade reading achievement beyond the prediction of intelligence or reading readiness scores.[66]

Although the research investigations of the 1960's have indicated that a relationship exists between self-concept and reading achievement, the findings of more recent studies do not tend to be as positive of this conclusion. To date investigations of the question of causation are limited in number and inconclusive in their findings.

Presently there is a growing interest in the effect of teacher attitude and behavior on the child's self-concept. This chapter continues with a presentation of research in this area.

The Teacher and Self-Concept

The child enters school with a wide assortment of ideas about himself and his abilities. However, he is by no means a simplified personality with singular traits, feelings, ideas and attitudes. Therefore, these are critical years. His self-concept is still in process, subject to the effects of every experience, including those in the classroom. Combs comments: "Outside the child's own family, no institution in our society is in a better position to affect the growth and development of an individual's self-image than our public schools." [67]

Much concern has been expressed about the personal development of the individual child within the context of formal education. Yet it would appear that there is a vast difference between what the teacher desires to do and what she actually does to enhance the child's human development.[68] If one accepts the fact that the teacher is also a significant person in the development of the child's self-concept, it follows that the perceptions which the teacher holds of children are critical. Moustakas [69] and Purkey[70] posit that the teacher must view children in essentially positive ways, if positive self-concepts are to develop.

In 1960, Davidson and Lang investigated, among other factors, the relationship between students' perceptions of their teachers' feelings toward them and the children's self-perception. A Check List of Trait Names, which consisted of 35 descriptive terms, was administered to 114 boys and 89 girls in grades 4, 5 and 6 of a New York public school. The children were also rated by their teachers on a number of behavioral characteristics. When the data was analyzed, the researchers found that there was a positive and significant correlation between the children's perception of their teachers' feelings toward them and the children's self-perceptions. The children with the more favorable self-concepts were those who more likely than not perceived their teachers' feelings toward them as favorable.[71]

The results of this study are most impressive when one considers a later body of research which investigated the nature of teachers' appraisal of children's self-concepts. In 1965, Lo Presti sought to determine the extent of reliance that could be placed on teacher judgment relative to appraisals of pupil personal and social adjustment. A Pupil Adjustment Inventory was designed by the researcher and completed by twenty-seven teachers. The 644 students in their respective classrooms were tested by means of the California Test of Personality and another researcher designed instrument entitled, About Myself. Analysis of scores derived on the three instruments employed resulted in a positive but low correlation.[72]

Seig, in 1972, explored teacher-student congruency and its relationship to reading achievement in grades 4, 5 and 6. She also queried whether teachers see their students in the same way as students see themselves. After her investigation of 138 students was completed, she determined that good readers' and poor readers' self-perceptions did not differ as widely as did their teachers' perceptions of them.[73]

A comparison of teacher and student perceptions of interpersonal relationships and self-concepts was undertaken by Jones. Results of her research not only confirmed the hypothesis that there was a significant relationship between students' perception of their self-concepts and their perception of the teacher-student interpersonal relationships but also that teachers were significantly inaccurate in approximating students' self-concepts.[74]

There are a number of studies, however, which suggest that teacher inability in this area can be overcome through increased knowledge of child development, a fuller appreciation of self-concept growth and development and sensitivity training.

In 1958 Perkins studied the value of teacher participation in an in-service child study program as it related to the teachers' perception of children's self-concepts. A representative sample consisting of students from four fourth grade classrooms and four sixth grade classrooms was selected for purposes of this research project. The four teachers at the sixth grade level, who had completed a three year in-service child study program sponsored by the Institute for Child Study at the University of Maryland, were compared with teachers who had never participated in this program. Perkins concluded: 1) that teacher participation in child study courses significantly increased the teacher's ability to assess the child's self-concept, and 2) children in the classrooms of these teachers were also far more able to assess the self-concepts of their peers.[75] In a similar study reported later in that same year Perkins corroborated his earlier findings.[76]

Bolea attempted to determine whether changes in the self-concepts of children accompany teacher participation in child study programs. The results of his work with fourth and sixth grade children indicated that change did occur in the self-concept of children toward developing a positive self-regard when their teachers were involved in child study.[77]

In 1973, Brown investigated the impact of teacher consultation on the self-perceptions of elementary school children. Teachers in the experimental group were provided an opportunity to observe their own classroom behavior via video tape and to participate in a program designed to illustrate how their behavior influences the classroom learning environment and the child's self-concept. After six weeks in-service education, the researcher observed significant and positive changes in the children's sense of personal worth and adequacy.[78]

Conflicting results were obtained by Baraffi who provided a series of sensitizing exercises for teachers. These exercises, based on a child study program, were designed to develop a fuller understanding of the meaning of human behavior and what is required to facilitate their own positive full development and that of their students. The investigator found no significant change in either the total self-concept or in the subordinate areas of physical, affectional, per group or the self-adjustive self-concept of the migrant children with whom these teachers worked.[79]

Positive feelings about self can be acquired simultaneously with the general curriculum in the regular instructional program. An experiment undertaken by Staines has shown that self-actualization can be achieved in classroom with no loss of learning of traditional subject matter. He studied two matched fourth grade classrooms where each teacher pursued her normal routine and curriculum. In addition the experimental teacher attempted to help children explore and build positive self-concepts. At the end of the year, the two groups were on a par academically, but the mental health scores of the children taught by the teacher who was concerned about self-concept increased significantly.[80]

Combs posits that teachers must not only be aware of the importance of the self-concept but they must also be willing to admit concern about self-concept and find ways of creating a climate in the classroom that will permit discovery and exploration of the self. In addition, they must find ways of actively encouraging the student's self in a positive direction. It is essential that teachers be fully aware of the following considerations: a) each person is worthy of respect; b) that each grows continuously from birth to death, at all times merging the past and future into the now; c) that each is a product of an inner core developed and modified by experience; d) that interaction with people is the strongest environmental determinant in the self-concept; e) that when the environment is basically unthreatening, the individual's own behavior toward elements in the environment is basically open, interactive and constructive; and f) that in this environment dignity and integrity emerge as characteristics of people.[81]

Kunz reviewed a portion of the literature relating to self-concept and reading. In this instance she cited several studies on the role of self-concept as it relates to the young child's learning to read. She concluded her review with the following statement:

> Teachers are indeed significant adults who can be instrumental in accomplishing the goal of increasing sensitivity to, and perceptions of, their own self-concepts and those of others as they teach children the tools of reading.[82]

Existing data have demonstrated that teachers appraise the child's self-concept incorrectly. However, skill in this area can be developed through in-service education in child development and sensitivity training. This increased knowledge and understanding is also reflected in the teacher's greater awareness of the impact of self-concept and a willingness to attend to this aspect of the child's growth in the classroom. Next, this chapter considers the effects of teacher behavior and teacher attitude on reading achievement.

The Teacher and Reading Achievement

The classic study of Rosenthal and Jacobson,[83] commonly referred to as *Pygmalion in the Classroom*, supported the premise that teachers often adjust their behavior to respond to a child's IQ. In this study, the researchers chose the names of first grade children at random and informed their classroom teachers that these children would grow dramatically in academic areas as well as mental ability during the coming school year. Subsequent testing indicated that the experimental group gained an average of 12.0 IQ points compared to an average gain of 8.4 IQ points for the control group. Interestingly enough, the experimental group was viewed by their teachers as being better adjusted, happier and possessing a better chance for academic success than the control children. Rosenthal and Jacobson concluded that the teacher, through her verbal and non-verbal behavior toward the experimental group, subtly helped them to learn. In summarizing their study, the researchers state: "Children who are expected to gain intellectually by their teachers in fact do show greater gains after one year, than do children of whom such gains are not expected."[84]

Although several subsequent replications of this research undertaken by such investigators as: Evans; Flemming; Goldsmith; Wilkins; and Spielberg[85] did not substantiate the findings of Rosenthal and Jacobson, the results of that study stimulated tremendous interest in the whole area of teacher expectations and their resultant effects on student achievement. In 1968, Weintraub stated, "The research reviewed and conducted by Rosenthal and others poses some intriguing questions for reading instruction.[86]

Other research data which assisted in directing reading researchers' interests toward the teacher and away from materials and modes of instruction was that produced by the First Grade Reading Study. This massive place of research consisting of twenty-seven independent studies, planned, directed and implemented by nationally known leaders in the field of reading was an attempt to explore the effects of various approaches to beginning reading on children's reading achievement. The results of this study suggest that the methodology and materials employed are comparatively incidental. Bond writes, "As would be expected, there was greater variation between the teachers within the method than there was between the methods."[87]

This concept was also substantiated by Harris and Morrison in the final portion of the CRAFT Project report, in which they state, "...the results of the study here, indicated that the teacher is far more important than the method."[88]

As a result of these studies, current reports of research in reading evidence an increase in studies of teacher expectation, teacher attitude and teacher personality.

In the area of teacher expectation particular emphasis has been placed on the possible effects of teacher expectancies on the reading achievement of boys since the majority of problems are among the male population. To date results of these investigations are in conflict.

In 1969 Good, after carefully observing differential teacher behaviors, types of feedback provided and the quality of children's responses, found that teachers extend equal treatment to boys and girls. However, high achieving students of both sexes receive preferential treatment in some instances.[89] Conversely Schell, as a result of his study of sex bias in teacher assessment of reading achievement, concluded that there was no convincing evidence of systematic, large scale teacher bias.[90]

Studies which report a definite difference in teacher expectation for boys with a resultant effect on their reading achievement were reported by Palardy and Doyle. In the former study Palardy concluded, as a result of his investigation of sixty-three first grade teachers, that when first grade teachers believed that boys were less successful than girls in learning to read, the boys did achieve less well on standardized reading tests.[91] In the latter investigation, Doyle, who collected data on eleven first grade teachers and their students, determined that there was strong evidence between sex linked teacher perceptions and reading achievement.[92]

Although their study was not specifically related to reading achievement, Aspy and Roebuck presented interesting findings regarding the relationship between student levels of cognitive functioning and teachers' classroom behavior. As a result of their work with forty teachers and the large number of children represented in their classrooms, an analysis of their findings suggests that a teacher's increased positive regard for students is translated into classroom behavior which elicits higher levels of cognitive functioning.[93]

In an investigation of teaching behavior and the reading performance of below-average readers, Samph studied 155 sixth grade students who were reading two or more years below grade level. These students were grouped according to the type of verbal behavior their teachers manifested, as determined by the Flanders system of interaction analysis. Analysis of his data suggested that below-average achievers, who had indirect teachers, not only showed more positive attitudes but also showed increased gains in achievement.[94]

Two recent studies have investigated the effect of teacher personality on reading achievement. In 1970, McDaniel found no significant differences between teacher personality groups and kindergarten children's scores on the Metropolitan Reading Readiness Test.[95] Moreover, the research of Bazemore in 1971, who worked with fifty-nine children in grades 3 through 6 who were enrolled in a summer reading program indicated no significant differences in the reading achievement of the children who worked with the warm, helping-type teacher as compared to the children who worked with the teacher who assumed an authority figure role.[96]

These findings however, were not substantiated by Chall and Feldman who undertook a research investigation to determine the personal characteristics and abilities of the effective teacher of first grade reading. The instructional and organizational approaches which the researchers found significant were: 1) ecclectic methods; 2) selection and presentation of appropriate lessons; 3) attention to individual differences; and 4) encouragement of pupil participation. They also concluded that the teachers who felt at ease and exhibited warmth toward the children were usually successful.[97]

In a study comparing a language-experience approach with a skills-centered approach, Harris and his collaborators found that teachers in the former method received good results with praise and poor results with criticism. Teachers in the skills-centered approach seemed to elicit better results when they avoided excessive praise or criticism and concentrated on skills instruction.

From other studies Harris drew these conclusions:

1. Mild criticism does not seem to affect achievement, but strong criticism negatively affects achievement

2. No relation between the frequency of use of praise and achievement has been found.

3. Praise seems to be more effective when issued in relation to a specific student contribution.[98]

Prows endeavored to determine whether a reading consultant, through working with teachers in the classroom, could assist teachers in becoming more sensitive to the child's self-concept. She also queried whether teachers would be willing to change their methods and procedures in an attempt to build positive self-concepts in children and as a result increase their reading achievement. Three classrooms were selected for purposes of the study. The two experimental teachers both received sensitivity training. However, one was instructed to use an individualized approach in teaching reading while the other employed the traditional three group approach. As a result of her study, Prows concluded that teachers can be trained to become more sensitive to their students. This also was evidenced by the fact that the teacher of the three group approach gradually moved into an individualized approach as her sensitivity to her students increased.[99]

An analysis of the findings of the research cited suggests that:
1) teacher behavior and teacher attitude do affect reading achievement, and
2) teachers are willing to modify their methods of reading instruction in an attempt to build positive self-concepts in children. Another dimension which is of importance is classroom organization. This area will be considered in the subsequent pages.

Classroom Organization, Reading Achievement and Self-Concept

Several approaches to school organization have been and still are being utilized in an attempt to meet the needs of individual children. These include homogeneous grouping, team teaching, non-graded classrooms and multi-age grouping. However, since the present study is concerned with classroom organization, this portion of the review of research will focus on organizations which are utilized in self-contained, heterogeneously grouped classrooms for purposes of reading instruction. The two most commonly employed organizational approaches in this category are ability groups wherein a basal reader is generally used and the individualized reading approach.[100]

Individualized Reading and Ability Groups.

As individualized reading became increasingly popular in the late 1950's and throughout the 1960's many educators queried whether this or the ability groups approach was more effective. As a result many invesitgations compared these two types of organization.

Studies in Support of the Individualized Reading Approach

McChristey conducted a year-long study of 160 second grade children who were matched on the basis of reading ability, years of attendance, age and socio-economic background. The eight teachers were also equated on their background, experience and competence. Four experimental groups were taught by the individualized plan, while the four control groups were taught in three groups with the use of basal readers. Both groups had access to many attractive library books for supplementary reading. At the conclusion of the study, the control group averaged 1.14 years in total reading gains, while the experimental group averaged 1.41 years. In vocabulary growth, the control group averaged 1.09 years and the experimental 1.96 years. In comprehension 59 percent of the experimental group gained two years or more, while only 24 percent of the control group scored in this range.[101]

Cynog[102] compared the reading achievement scores of pupils who had been taught consistently within the framework of an individualized reading program from the first through the sixth grade with the scores obtained by children using the basal approach in the same school district over a similar period of time. Test results were compared on the third, fourth, fifth and sixth grade levels. The results of her survey indicate that the children who were taught under the individualized reading plan made conspicuously higher scores than did the rest of the children in the district. Cynog concluded: "There are some indications that the longer the children received individualized reading instruction, the more rapid did their achievement in reading accelerate.[103]

In a comparative study by Acinapuro the children in three individualized reading classes were compared to those in three basal reading classrooms on the basis of growth in achievement, interest and attitude over a ten month period. These groups were equated on the following variables: grade, age, intelligence, sex and socio-economic factors. Teachers were also matched on: education beyond the bachelor's degree, experience within the grade presently taught, general educational philosophy, willingness to enter the study and satisfaction with their assignments in the study. Test results showed both groups to be equally efficient in reading vocabulary. However, the scores of the individualized reading group were statistically significant in their superiority over the basal group in silent reading comprehension and general reading achievement. There was no evidence to indicate that individualized reading fostered a more favorable attitude toward reading.[104]

A carefully controlled study of the program of 259 first grade children in 14 experimental classrooms and 208 first grades in 14 control classrooms over a three-year period was undertaken by Johnson.[105] All experimental classes were paired with control classrooms located either in the same school or community in an effort to establish some control over socio-economic conditions. A concentrated effort was made to equalize class size, time spent in reading instruction and materials. Continuous in-service was provided for both groups of teachers. Test results at the end of the first year showed that the children in the individualized classroom scored slightly, but significantly, higher in word knowledge, word discrimination and comprehension than the children in the basal group. By the end of the third year, the differences were even less, but still significant. Johnson summarized his findings as follows: "Clearly the results of this study indicate that pupils can achieve at least as well and perhaps even better than pupils in the basal reader program in individualized classrooms.[106]

Teigland reported an experiment in which entering first grade children in three schools were randomly assigned to either a basal reading classroom, or one in which an individualized approach was used. At the end of second grade, data were available on 65 pupils in the basal approach group and 69 pupils in the individualized approach group. When the California Reading Test was administered at the end of second grade, the individualized reading group had significantly higher scores on comprehension than the basal group, the vocabulary scores favored the individualized group but were not significant. The quality, variety and difficulty of books read favored the individualized approach to a highly significant degree.[107]

Studies Indicating No Significant Differences between the Two Approaches

An interesting study was presented by Bonhorst and Sellers.[108] During an entire school year, five of the six primary grade teachers in one school in Atlanta, Georgia made preparations for and participated in an experiment which involved their more capable students. Each taught according to the basal program for the first half of the year. Meanwhile, each teacher prepared for the experiment by reading extensively in the area of individualized reading and laying careful plans for the implementation of the program in her classroom. The latter part of the school year (mid-January through the middle of May) was divided into two periods of eight weeks. In one period each teacher taught the regular basal approach and in the other an individualized approach was utilized with the selected students. Test results for each of these periods were compared. This comparison gave a suggestion of better progress for the experimental approach but the differences were not significant. Bonhorst and Sellers concluded that, "The findings were tentative at best."[109]

A doctoral study conducted by Walker involved two groups of carefully matched children in grades four, five and six. Controls included reading ability, IQ and socio-economic status. Both groups of children were taught by student teachers under the supervision of critic teachers. The control group followed a basal reader approach, while the experimental group engaged in individualized reading. The data showed no significant differences between the groups in reading scores. However, the children in the experimental situation did exhibit a greater interest in reading and consequently read more books.[110]

In an effort to compare the effects of an individualized reading approach on the word identification abilities of first grade children, Izzo established experimental and control groups consisting of 68 children each from 8 first grade classrooms. Both groups were considered comparable in readiness, kindergarten experience, age, sex and teacher qualifications. Results of testing after a seven-month period showed no significant differences in the relative effectiveness of the two methods.[111]

In a companion study, Bradford studied the same population as Izzo. Her purpose, however, was to compare the effectiveness of these two approaches in developing comprehension skills. As a result of testing, also done at the end of seven months, she found there were no significant differences between the two approaches. Although the range of achievement was similar in both groups, she found the group approach to be more effective in helping children achieve at a rate consistent with their mental ability.[112]

Adams reports a study in which a total of 172 first grade children were involved. Eighty-four pupils were taught using individualized reading and 88 using a modified basal approach for a total of 102 days. She found no significant differences between the achievement of the two groups.[113]

Possibly one of the most carefully controlled studies that has been done in comparing individual and group procedures is that reported by Sartain.[114] Five of ten classes of second graders were taught for 56 school days by means of an individualized approach, while the other five classes were taught by a program incorporating basal readers as well as an extensive program of voluntary reading. At the end of the first period the teachers who had taught individualized reading changed to the basal program and vice versa. Evaluations of the progress were made by means of standardized tests, and appraisals of strengths and weaknesses of the individualized program were secured through teacher judgments.

Sartain's analysis of his findings indicate that, "The individualized method does not produce better reading gains than a strong basal program..."[115] He found, too, that capable students made approximately the same gains in reading with both approaches. He stated, however, that because of the efficiency of instruction and provision made through basal materials for systematic growth, both basal and supplementary materials should be retained for the capable as well as the slower students. Sartain concluded that one of the strong features of the individualized program was the individual conference with the pupils. Consequently, he recommends the incorporation of this feature into the basal program.[116]

Studies in Support of the Ability Group Approach

Karr reports the results of an experiment in Pittsburg, California, in which third graders were taught by an individualized approach which utilized pupil-teachers in assisting the slower learners for six months. The children in the experimental group were limited in the number of books they read above the third grade level and were not allowed to read in the basal series used throughout the school. At the end of a six month-period, they were compared with children in another California community who had been taught by group procedures by teachers who were quite eqger to improve their teaching techniques. Tests results indicated that the children in the group situation had significantly higher gains in vocabulary and comprehension. Nonetheless, the teachers in the individualized program expressed satisfaction with the plan.[117]

Anderson, Hughes and Dixon compared the performance of pupils in a University laboratory school in which the individualized reading approach was used with that of the pupils in a neighboring school who were very systematically taught by the basal approach. Although the average IQ of the children in the control group was ten points lower than that of the children in the experimental situation, the findings of this five year study indicated that a far greater percentage of the basal group achieved a reading age of 84 months at or before the same chronological age. The brighter group did not overtake the basal group until they were 132 months old or eleven years of age.[118]

In an effort to eliminate all possibilities of the halo effect, which he feels grossly distorts the findings of much research, Safford[119] made a study of 7 classrooms (grades 3 through 8) in which 183 pupils had been taught for the previous 3 years by the self-selection technique. The mean class increments were compared with national and district norms after the individual growth of each child, as well as the mean growth of the 7 classrooms were computed. The results of this comparison showed that none of the individualized classes came close to the national norm gain of 1.0 nor the district gain of 1.25. Safford concluded:

> For the majority of individual pupils in the 7 classes, the use of individualized reading techniques resulted in lower gains in reading achievement over a period of one calendar year.[120]

Individualized Reading and Self-Concept

Two studies were undertaken in the 1970's to investigate the effect of group reading instruction and individualized reading instruction on self-concept and reading achievement. For purposes of his study, Marani selected 36 fifteen year old boys who were classified as uncontrollable, juvenile delinquents. Twelve were assigned to an experimental group in which reading was taught by means of individualized instruction. Twelve were assigned to another experimental group in which the traditional small group approach was utilized and the remaining twelve were assigned to a control situation. After a lapse of eight weeks and 30 periods of reading instruction, Marani found no significant difference between the two approaches in either self-concept or reading achievement.[121] The results of this study were substantiated by those of Marble who also studied this question with a group of fifth grade children.[122]

In summary the research on individualized reading is inconclusive. While some studies support this approach to classroom organization, others do not. A few studies have indicated that there is no relationship between individualized instruction in reading and self-concept. Another way of approaching the teaching of reading is through a total reorganization of the classroom in all its aspects. This approach is exemplified in the activity-centered classroom.

The Activity-Centered Classroom

The fact that the concept of the activity-centered classroom is not a new one is evidenced by Wallen and Travers' presentation and critique of a number of studies undertaken between 1923 and 1958 which investigated the effect of this approach to classroom organization on achievement. In this review, the authors report that they found no important differences in terms of subject matter mastery among children who attended these classrooms.[123] They cite, "...a superiority in terms of the characteristics which the progressive schools seek to develop...initiativeness, work, spirit and critical thinking.[124]

During the late 1960's attempts were made to evaluate the open concept approach to education. However, it is not this researcher's intent to present these studies, as they generally were conducted in open space schools and the focal point of this study is the activity-centered, self-contained classroom.

Reading Instruction in the Informal Classroom

Until very recently there had been no published surveys on the materials and approaches used in the informal classroom in either England or the United States. In February 1974, Weiner reported the results of her investigation of 280 informal, open classroom teachers in Wassau and Suffolk counties of Long Island, New York. The results of her survey indicated that:

1. The traditional, three, fixed reading group approach was rarely used, and had been replaced by temporary, flexible groupings for specific skills instruction.

2. Generally the approach to reading was individualized. However, the teacher provided many direct lessons in the skills areas.

3. The study skills were most frequently integrated with content area research projects.

4. A wide variety of reading materials including: basals; programmed materials; language-experience stories; workbooks and tradebooks was utilized.

5. Children had free and easy access to library materials which were used for both pleasure and research pupposes.

6. These American teachers set aside far more time for reading than their British counterparts. In fact, 90 percent of the respondents provided direction and structure and 66 percent set time aside, precisely for reading instruction.[125]

Weiner concluded her report as follows: "...it is encouraging to note that the open classroom has provided change not only in the structure of the classroom but also in philosophy, methodology and instruction.[126]

Although the second survey is an older one, it has only recently been reported in this country by Weintraub in the Reading Research Quarterly. This survey, undertaken by Goodacre, studied among other factors the methods and materials used in one hundred of Britain's infant and junior schools which were representative of the London primary schools. Results of this survey indicated that:

1. Contrary to the thinking of many Americans 73 percent of the schools were described as informal and 13 percent tended to be formal

2. The major methods of teaching reading were alphabetic, phonic, whole-word and sentence.

3. While 35 reception class teachers stated that they did not teach phonics, 37 indicated that they taught phonics and 26 remarked that phonics instruction was provided for some children only.

4. A large number of the schools (82) used a basal series to teach reading, however, the majority of the schools (88) supplemented their basals with readers from other series

5. Only 43 of the 100 schools surveyed used standardized achievement tests[127]

Reading Achievement in the Informal Classroom

There is an apparent paucity of research on the topic of reading achievement in the type of activity-centered classrooms which follow the British Infant School model. Most of the available research in this area comes from England where informal education has been in existence since the end of World War II. These British studies have been reviewed and critiqued in the writing of Silberman, Beller, Goddard, Southgate and Weiner.[128]

In 1967, the Central Advisory committee presented a review of primary education in England. Included in this report was a presentation of the data obtained on reading achievement from 1948-1964. The report stated that according to standardized tests, administered periodically by the Department of Education and Science throughout this twenty-six year period, eleven year old children in 1964 were reading approximately seventeen months above the level reached by eleven year olds in 1948. Moreover in 1964, the eleven year olds were reading almost at the same level as the thirteen year olds had in 1948. Furthermore, the median level of competence reached by half of the children in 1948 was reached by three-quarters of the eleven year olds in 1964.[129]

Silberman writes:

> This conclusion is confirmed by several studies which have compared the reading attainment of matched groups of students in informal and formal schools and found no significant differences between the two at either the infant or junior school level.[130]

Three studies suggest the positive effect of the informal school, not only in reading but also in other areas of growth. In summarizing her study, Lowell states:

> Overall there is no evidence whatever of any deterioration of reading standards in informal Junior Schools. Although there is no evidence that these schools bring superior standards of reading, they may well benefit their pupils in other ways.[131]

Lovell's findings corroborated those of an earlier study of Gardner, who was one of the first researchers to compare the results of formal and informal infant schools. In this investigation she found that ten year olds, who had attended informal infant schools, tended to be superior to children who had had a formal school experience.[132]

In addition, Warburton, as cited by Southgate, concluded that the main benefit of progressive or informal education appeared to be in preventing backwardness in reading.[133]

Gardner also conducted a twelve year longitudinal study in which she: 1) compared the progress of students in seven traditional infant schools with that of children in seven informal infant schools, and 2) compared the development of students in twelve traditional junior schools with that of children in twelve informal junior schools. Measures of reading achievement were available for only two pairs of infant schools however, and here the traditional schools were superior. Conversely, complete data were available for all students in the twelve pairs of junior schools. In this instance the children in the traditional schools were somewhat ahead in both mechanical arithmetic and arithmetic problem-solving, while the children in the experimental schools were somewhat ahead in reading. She also noted that children from the informal classrooms generally showed less anxiety, more initiative, independence and self-confidence.[134]

In commenting on these studies Beller states:

It is clear from these findings, with the exception of certain specific skills such as reading at the end of infant school and arithmetic at the end of junior school, the experimental or child-centered educational programs resulted in superiority on most attitude as well as attainment measures.[135]

Harckman hypothesized that on a theoretical basis children who were in a warm, comfortable setting, learning at their own rate, have an advantage in learning to read. Three samples were tested: 187 inner-London children; 13 pairs of siblings in a suburban London school and 47 children in a suburban junior school. In all three instances, reading achievement was measured by the Holborn Reading Analysis Test. Analysis of the data revealed higher means for children in the informal schools, but a significant difference was found only in the case of the inner London schools.[136]

The results of three investigations however, do not corroborate the findings of the research cited above. In 1959, Morris after analyzing the test results of children seven to eleven years of age concluded that good reading achievement is associated with a formal approach to reading and a particular emphasis on phonics.[137] In addition, Cane and Smithers, who collected data on students in twelve infant schools from depressed areas, found that initial reading success was not achieved in the informal classrooms.[138] Finally, are the conclusions gathered as a result of a National Foundation Reading Survey which were published in 1972. These findings indicated that in contrast to the earlier statements of the Central Advisory Committee regarding reading achievement from 1948-1964, average test scores are now falling off. One decisive result of these findings is that the Secretary of State of Education has created a special committee to inquire into the teaching or reading.[139]

In summary the research on the activity-centered approach has been confined to England. Earlier studies reported an increase in reading achievement but more recent research reveals a downward trajectory in reading scores. This investigator has discovered no empirical data on self-concept and reading achievement in the informal classroom. The present study is an attempt to investigate the relationship between self-concept and classroom organization as it is modeled after the British Infant Schools and reading achievement.

CHAPTER SUMMARY

Emotions, Personality and Reading Achievement

A number of investigators have attempted to examine the nature of the relationship between emotions, personality and reading achievement. Although the findings of these studies generally indicate that there is a relationship between these factors, the question of causality remains unanswered. Whether reading problems are the cause of emotional problems or whether emotional problems are the cause of reading disabilities has been commented upon as recently as 1972. Heilman wrote:

> It is apparent from the literature on emotions and reading that there are two major hypotheses which might account for the interactions between emotions and reading...
> (1) When emotional problems and reading problems are found together, the emotional problem stems from failure, frustration, tension and pressure connected with reading problems.
> (2) Unresolved emotional problems, which need not have been related to reading, may prevent the child from applying his energies to the learning task. The non-reading behavior is simply a symptom of the emotional problem.[140]

More recently, Harris, after reviewing many of the studies conducted in this area, commented:

> In general disabled readers tend to be more dependent, more insecure and less socially mature; however whether these are causes or effects of reading disability has yet to be determined. Obviously this is an area where further research is needed.[141]

Self-Concept and Reading Achievement

Although the research of the 1960's generally suggests that there is a relationship between self-concept and reading, the findings of the more recent studies tend to question this conclusion. The differences might be due to the fact that the older studies examined this relationship in older children, who because of their added years in school would have experienced a great many more successful and unsuccessful experiences in reading. The research which has explored the possibility of self-concept as a causative factor is inconclusive and limited. A comparison of the older and more recent research studies, with their conflicting outcomes, accentuates the compelling need for further research.

The Teacher and Self-Concept

The inadequacy of teachers to accurately assess the child's self-concept has been clearly demonstrated. However, through in-service training and child study programs it has been shown that teachers can learn to become more sensitive to the development of the child's self-concept, and help children to develop more positive pictures of themselves. It is obvious that there are implications here for teacher training and that variations in the preparation and training of teachers may produce significant differences in their ability to influence the development of positive self-concepts.

The Teacher and Reading Achievement

It may be hypothesized that the paucity of research on the effective teacher of reading is due to the fact that until recently more emphasis was placed on techniques and materials of reading instruction. The available research, however, suggests that the teacher--her warmth, personality, verbal behavior, expectations and regard for students is of importance. It also has been suggested that sensitivity to the self-concepts of children can be increased to the extent that teachers will willingly modify their methods of reading instruction in an attempt to simultaneously build positive self-concepts.

Individualized Instruction, Reading Achievement and Self-Concept

It is evident from the research cited, that there is a pattern of conflicting findings. A few studies provide evidence that children made better gains with the individualized approach; a few supported the grouping approach, while many indicated no significant differences in reading achievement between the two approaches. Additionally neither of the recent investigations which studied self-concept and individualized instruction found that self-concept was enhanced when this approach was used. To further confuse the issue, many valid questions have been raised by noted authorities regarding the longevity, reliability, validity and control of much of the research in this area.[142]

Nevertheless, the practice has been approved by many educators. It appears that Heathers' comment is noteworthy.

> Writing an epitaph for grouping may well be the task of the reviewer of research on grouping for the 1980 edition of this encyclopedia. Even today it appears that grouping as a central theme for instruction has nearly run its course and is in the process of being replaced by a familiar theme--individualized instruction that became a focus of educational reform in the mid-1960's.[143]

The Activity-Centered Classroom and Reading Achievement

Although the earlier investigations of reading achievement in the informal classroom have presented positive findings, the more current researchers are concluding that reading achievement is on the decline in these classrooms. To date this investigator has not located reports on the nature of the effect of the activity-centered, self-contained classroom organization on self-concept.

Conclusions

The following conclusions may be drawn from the research cited in this chapter:

1. Since the more recent research does not seem to corroborate the findings of older investigations regarding the nature of the relationship between self-concept and reading achievement there is a clear need to investigate this area further. Such studies would be facilitated by a uniform definition of the word "self-concept" and the development of more valid and reliable instruments for self-concept measurement.

2. Teachers who have been trained and who have learned to become more aware

of the development of the child as well as more cognizant of their impact as teachers on the child's self-concept seem to provide classroom experiences which foster the growth of positive self-concepts.

3. The teacher as a person and teacher expectations, attitude and personality are important variables affecting reading achievement.

4. To date research on individualized reading has not definitely shown that this is the one best organizational plan for improving reading and enhancing the self-concept. It may well be that what is needed is a total reorganization of the classroom, in which reading is but one of the subjects learned.

5. Many American educators are incorporating the informal approach as modeled after the British Infant Schools without a knowledge of its effect on the American child's self-concept or his reading achievement. This approach to education also has attracted considerable public attention. In this age of accountability it is obvious that research on this question is imperative.

6. The informal approach as examplified in the activity-centered classroom incorporates in a deliberate and conscious way concern about the influence of classroom organization and the teacher's training on the development of reading competence and positive self-concepts. An empirical comparison of the activity-centered approach with the traditional approach to classroom organization has heuristic value in generating new perspectives on the teaching of reading and the enrichment of the self-concept.

Chapter III describes the design and methodology employed by this researcher to investigate the problem, "A Study of the Relationship of Self-Concept and Classroom Organization to Reading Achievement in Grade One."

Footnotes:

11. Marion Monroe, Children Who Cannot Learn to Read (Chicago: University of Chicago Press, 1928), p. 105.

12. Marion Monroe, "Diagnosis and Treatment of Reading Disabilities", Educational Diagnosis in Thirty-fourth Yearbook of the National Society for the Study of Education, pt. 1 (Bloomington, Ill.: Public School Publishing Co., 1935), pp. 201-228.

13. Marion Monroe and B. Backus, Remedial Reading: A Monograph in Character Education (Boston: Houghton Mifflin Co., 1937).

14. Phyllis Blanchard, "Reading Disabilities in Relation to Maladjustment, "Mental Hygiene 12 (July 1928):775.

15. Phyllis Blanchard, "Reading Disabilities in Relation to Difficulties of Personality and Emotional Development", Mental Hygiene 20 (July 1936):412.

16. Phyllis Blanchard, "Psychoanalytic Contributions to the Problems of Reading Difficulties," The Psychoanalytic Study of the Child 2 (April 1946):163-187.

17. Arthur I. Gates, "The Role of Personality Maladjustment in Reading Disability", Journal of Genetic Psychology 59 (June 1941):82.

18. David H. Russell, "Research on Reading Difficulty and Personality", Official Report of the American Educational Research Association, in Improving Educational Research (Washington, D.C.: American Educational Research Association, 1948), p.12.

19. Nila B. Smith, "Research on Reading and Emotions," School and Society 81 (January 1955):10.

20. Jules C. Abrams, "A Study of Certain Personality Characteristics of Non-Readers and Achieving Readers", Dissertation Abstracts, 16 (Ann Arbor, Michigan: University Microfilms, a Xerox Company, 1956), pp. 377-378.

21. B. E. Tabarlett, "Poor Readers and Mental Health", Elementary English 35 (December 1958):526.

22. Ralph D. Norman and Marvin F. Daley, "The Comparative Personality Adjustment of Superior and Inferior Readers", Journal of Educational Psychology 50 (February 1959):35.

23. Marvin Powell and Jerry Bergen, "An Investigation of Differences Between Tenth-, Eleventh-, and Twelfth-Grade 'Conforming and Nonconforming' Boys", The Journal of Educational Research 56 (December 1962); 184-190.

24. Glen M. Chronister, "Personality and Reading Achievement", Elementary School Journal 64 (February 1964):253-260.

25. William S. Durr and Robert R. Schmatz, "Personality Differences Between High-Achieving Gifted Children", The Reading Teacher 17 (January 1964):251-254.

26. Irla Zimmerman and George Allebrand, Personality Characteristics and Attitudes Toward Achievement", The Journal of Educational Research 59 (September 1965): 28-30.

27. Barry P. Frost, "Some Personality Characteristics of Poor Readers", Psychology in the Schools 1-2 (July 1965):218-219.

28. Erwin Singer and Marion E. Pittman, "A Sullivanian Approach to the Problem of Reading Disability: Theoretical Considerations and Empirical Data", Journal of Projective Techniques and Personality Assessment 24 (September 1965):369-374.

29. Lily Schroeder, "A Study of the Relationship Between Five Descriptive Categories of Emotional Disturbance and Reading and Arithmetic Achievement", Exceptional Children 32 (April 1965):11-12.

30. Irene J. Athey, "Reading-Personality Patterns at the Junior High School Level", Dissertation Abstracts, 26 (Ann Arbor, Michigan: University of Microfilms, a Xerox Company, 1966), pp. 861-862.

31. Ibid., p. 862

32. Ibid.

33. Margalith Holzinger, "Personality and Behavioral Characteristics of Able and Less Able Readers of Elementary and School Age", Dissertation Abstracts, 28 (Ann Arbor, Michigan: University Microfilms, a Xerox Company, 1967-1968), pp. 4909-A-4910-A.

34. Bertha Stavrianos and Sylvia Landsman, "Personality Patterns of Deficient Readers with Perceptual-Motor Problems", Psychology in the Schools 6 (April 1969):109-123.

35. R. D. Savage, "Personality Factors and Academic Attainment in Junior High School Children", British Journal of Educational Psychology 36 (May 1966): 91-92.

36. Martin A. Shapiro, "Relationship Among Extroversion, Neuroticism, Academic Reading Achievement and Verbal Learning", Dissertation Abstracts 28 (Ann Arbor, Michigan: University Microfilms, a Xerox Company, 1967-1968), pp. 4915-A-4916-A.

37. D. Bruce Bell, Robert F. Anderson and Franklin D. Lewis, "Some Personality and Motivational Factors in Reading Retardation", The Journal of Educational Research 65 (January 1972):229-233.

38. Louise B. Ames and Richard N. Walker, "Prediction of Later Reading Ability from Kindergarten Rorschach and IQ Scores", The Journal of Educational Research 55 (December 1964):309-313.

39. Jerome Kagan, "Reflection-Impulsivity and Reading Ability in Primary Grade Children", Child Development 36 (1965):609-628.

40. Maslow, Motivation and Personality: Rogers, Client-Centered Therapy; Hamachek, Encounters: and Combs and Snygg, Individual Behavior.

41. George A. Hallock, "Attitudinal Factors Affecting Achievement in Reading", <u>Dissertation Abstracts</u>, 18 (Ann Arbor, Michigan: University Microfilms, a Xerox Company, 1958), p. 2061.

42. Raymond Bodwin, "The Relationship between Immature Self-Concept and Certain Educational Disabilities," <u>Dissertation Abstracts</u>, 19 (Ann Arbor, Michigan: University Microfilms, a Xerox Company, 1959), pp. 1645-1646.

43. Donovan Lumpkin, "The Relationship of Self-Concept to Achievement in Reading", <u>Dissertation Abstracts</u>, 19 (Ann Arbor, Michigan: University Microfilms, a Xerox Company, 1959), pp. 204-205.

44. Rose Frances Spicola, "An Investigation into Seven Correlates of Reading Achievement Including Self-Concept", <u>Dissertation Abstracts</u>, 21 (Ann Arbor, Michigan: University Microfilms, a Xerox Company, 1961), p. 2199.

45. Patricia Bricklin, "Self-Related Concepts and Aspiration Behavior of Achieving Readers and Two Types of Non-Achieving Readers", <u>Dissertation Abstracts</u>, 26 (Ann Arbor, Michigan: University Microfilms, a Xerox Company, 1965), p. 3484.

46. George J. Blackman, "A Clinical Study of the Personality Structure and Adjustment of Pupils Underachieving and Overachieving in Reading", (Ed.D. dissertation, Cornell University, 1965).

47. Frederick K. Schwyhart, "Exploration of the Self-Concept of Retarded Readers in Relation to Reading Achievement", <u>Dissertation Abstracts</u>, 28 (Ann Arbor, Michigan: a Xerox Company, 1967-1968), p. 1218-A.

48. Gladys Toller, "Certain Aspects of the Self-Evaluations Made by Achieving and Retarded Readers of Average and Above Average Intelligence", <u>Dissertation Abstracts</u>, 28 (Ann Arbor, Michigan: University Microfilms, a Xerox Company, 1967-1968), p. 976-A.

49. Robert L. Williams and Spurgeon Cox, "Self-Concept and School Achievement", <u>Personnel and Guidance Journal</u> 46 (January 1968):478-481.

50. William B. Paddleford, "The Influence of Socioeconomic Level, Sex and Ethnic Background Upon the Relationship Between Reading Achievement and Self-Concept", <u>Dissertation Abstracts</u>, 30 (Ann Arbor, Michigan: University Microfilms, a Xerox Company, 1969-1970), pp. 3330-A-3331-A.

51. Sophie Lovinger, <u>The Interplay of Some Ego Functions in Six Year Old Children</u> (Bethesda, Md.: ERIC Document Reproduction Service, ED 020 005, 1967).

52. Leslie Carlton, "A Report of Self-Directive Dramatization in the Regular Elementary Classroom and Relationships Discovered with Progress in Reading Achievement and Self-Concept Changes", <u>Dissertation Abstracts</u>, 24 (Ann Arbor, Michigan: University Microfilms, a Xerox Company, 1963-1964), pp. 3142-3143.

53. James M. Hake, "Covert Motivation of Good and Poor Readers", <u>The Reading Teacher</u> 22 (May 1969):731-738, 741.

54. Ruby N. Cummings, "A Study of the Relationships between Self-Concept and Reading Achievement at Third-Grade Level", <u>Dissertation Abstracts</u>, 31 (Ann Arbor, Michigan: University Microfilms, a Xerox Company, 1970-1971), p. 5195-A.

55. Darlene J. Swartz, *The Relationship of Self-Esteem to Reading Performance* (Bethesda, Md.: ERIC Document Reproduction Service, ED 006 723, 1972).

56. Oren Glick, "Some Social-Emotional Consequences of Early Inadequate Acquisition of Reading Skills", *Journal of Educational Psychology* 63 (June 1972) 253-257.

57. Joan M. Wood, "The Relationship of Self-Concept to Reading Comprehension, Word Meaning and Intelligence" (M. Ed. thesis, University of New Hampshire, 1972).

58. Cleo D. Carter, "The Relationship between Personality and Academic Achievement of Seven Year Olds" (Ed.D. dissertation, Indiana University, 1953).

59. Liston O. Nicholson, "The Relationship between Self-Concept and Reading Achievement", *Dissertation Abstracts*, 25 (Ann Arbor, Michigan: University Microfilms, a Xerox Company, 1965), p. 6063.

60. Nassir Sedarat, "Relationship of Achievement Motive, Ego Strength and Certain Aspects of Word Association to the Reading Ability of Intellectually Superior Pupils", *Dissertation Abstracts*, 28 (Ann Arbor, Michigan: University Microfilms, a Xerox Company, 1968), p. 4202-A.

61. Velma Ruhly, "A Study of the Relationship of Self-Concept, Socioeconomic Background and Psycholinguistic Abilities to Reading Achievement of Second Grade Males Reading in a Suburban Area", *Dissertation Abstracts*, 31 (Ann Arbor, Michigan: University Microfilms, a Xerox Company, 1971), p. 4560-A.

62. Ruth W. Lewis, "The Relationship of Self-Concept to Reading Achievement", *Dissertation Abstracts*, 34 (Ann Arbor, Michigan: University Microfilms, a Xerox Company, 1974), p. 3839-A.

63. George A. Giuliani, "The Relationship of Self-Concept and Verbal-Mental Ability to Levels of Reading Readiness Amongst Kindergarten Children", *Dissertation Abstracts*, 28 (Ann Arbor, Michigan: University Microfilms, a Xerox Company, 1968), p. 3866-A.

64. Mary Lamy, "Relationship of Self-Perceptions of Early Primary Children to Achievement in Reading," *Dissertation Abstracts*, 24 (Ann Arbor, Michigan: University Microfilms, a Xerox Company, 1963), pp. 628-629.

65. William Wattenberg and Clare Clifford, "Relations of Self-Concept to Beginning Achievement in Reading", *Child Development* 35 (June 1964):466-467.

66. Jean H. Williams, "The Relationship of Self-Concept and Reading Achievement in First Grade Children", The Journal of Educational Research 66 (April 1973): 378-380.

67. Arthur W. Combs, "New Horizons in Field Research", *Educational Leadership* 15 (February 1958):315-316.

68. Angelo V. Boy and Gerald J. Pine, *Expanding the Self: Personal Growth for Teachers* (Dubuque, Iowa: Wm. C. Brown Company, 1971), p. 2.

69. Clark Moustakas, *The Authentic Teacher* (Cambridge, Massachusetts: Howard A. Doyle Publishing Company, 1966), pp. 37-38.

70. Purkey, _Self-Concept_, p. 47.

71. Helen Davidson and Gerhard Lang, "Children's Perception of Their Teachers' Feelings toward Them Related to Self-Perception, School Achievement and Behavior," _Journal of Experimental Education_ 29 (December 1960):107-118.

72. Peter J. LoPresti, "Teacher's Appraisal of the Personal and Social Adjustment of Fourth, Fifth and Sixth Graders as Compared with Self-Evaluations by the Pupils", _Dissertation Abstracts_, 26 (Ann Arbor, Michigan: University of Microfilms, a Xerox Company, 1966), p. 5134.

73. Janet Seig, _Teacher-Student Congruency and Its Relationship to Reading Achievement_ (Bethesda, Md.: ERIC Document Reproduction Service, ED 064 698, 1972).

74. Sara R. Jones, "A Comparison of Teacher and Student Perceptions of Interpersonal Relationships and Self-Concepts", _Dissertation Abstracts_, 34 (Ann Arbor, Michigan: University Microfilms, a Xerox Company, 1974), p. 3873-A.

75. Hugh V. Perkins, "Teachers' and Peers' Perceptions of Children's Self-Concepts", _Child Development_ 29 (June 1958):203-220.

76. Hugh V. Perkins, "Factors Influencing Change in Children's Self-Concepts", _Child Development_ 29 (June 1958):221-230.

77. Angelo J. Boleo, "Relationship of Change in Children's Self-Concept to Teacher Participation in a Child Study Program", _Dissertation Abstracts_, 28 (Ann Arbor, Michigan: University Microfilms, a Xerox Company, 1967-1968), p. 4904-A.

78. Jeanette A. Brown, "The Impact of Teacher Consultation on the Self-Perceptions of Elementary Children", _Education_ 93 (April-May 1972): 339-345.

79. Gino Baraffi, "The Effect of Two Types of Summer School Intervention on Self-Concept and Academic Achievement of Children of Seasonal and Migrant Workers", _Dissertation Abstracts_, 31 (Ann Arbor, Michigan: University Microfilms, a Xerox Company, 1970-1971), pp. 6269-A-6270-A.

80. J. W. Staines, "The Self-Picture as a Factor in the Classroom", _British Journal of Educational Psychology_ 28 (June 1958):97-111.

81. Arthur Combs, "A Perceptual View of the Adequate Personality", Perceiving Behaving Becoming, _1962 Yearbook of the Association for Supervision and Curriculum Development_, (Washington, D.C.: National Education Association, 1962), pp. 50-64.

82. Jean A. Kunz, "The Self-Concept of the Young Child As He Learns to Read", in _Claremont Reading Conference, Thirty-Second Yearbook_, ed. Malcolm P. Douglas (Claremont, California: Claremont Graduate School Curriculum Laboratory, 1968), p. 122.

83. Robert Rosenthal and L. Jacobson, _Pygmalion in the Classroom: Teacher Expectations and Pupils' Intellectual Development_ (New York: Holt, Rinehart and Winston, Inc., 1969).

84. Ibid., p. 221

85. Judith T. Evans, *Interpersonal Self-Fulfilling Prophecies: Further Explorations from the Laboratory to the Classroom* (Bethesda, Md.: ERIC Document Reproduction Service, ED 014 900, 1969); Elyse S. Flemming, *Teacher Expectancy or My Fair Lady* (Bethesda, Md.: ERIC Document Reproduction Service, ED 038 183, 1970): Josephine Goldsmith, *The Effect of a High Expectancy on Reading Achievement and IQ of Students in Grade Ten* (Bethesda, Md.: ERIC Document Reproduction Service, ED 049 901, 1971); William E. Wilkins, *Teacher Expectations and Student Achievement, A Replication Extension, Final Report* (Bethesda, Md.: ERIC Document Reproduction Service, ED 080 567, 1973); and Deanna B. Spielberg, "Labeling, Teacher Expectation, Pupil Intelligence Level and Conditions of Learning" (Ed.D. dissertation, Boston University, 1973).

86. Samuel Weintraub, "Research: Teacher Expectations and Reading Performance", *The Reading Teacher* 22 (March 1968):557.

87. Guy L. Bond, "First Grade Reading Studies: An Overview", *Elementary English* 63 (May 1966): 468.

88. Albert J. Harris and Coleman Morrison, "The CRAFT Project: A Final Report", *The Reading Teacher* 22 (January 1969):340.

89. Thomas I. Good, *Do Boys and Girls Receive Equal Opportunity in First Grade Reading Instruction?* (Bethesda, Md.: ERIC Document Reproduction Service, ED 041, 848, 1969).

90. Leo M. Schell, *An Investigation of Sex Bias in Teacher Assessment of Reading Achievement of Elementary School Pupils* (Bethesda, Md.: ERIC Document Reproduction Service, ED 039 118, 1969).

91. J. Michael Palardy, "What Teachers Believe - What Children Achieve", *Elementary School Journal* 69 (April 1969):370-374.

92. Wayne J. Doyle, *Teacher Perceptions: Do They Make a Difference?* (Bethesda, Md.: ERIC Document Reproduction Service, ED 048, 109, 1971).

93. David N. Aspy and Flora M. Roebuck, "An Investigation of the Relationship Between Student Levels of Cognitive Functioning and the Teacher's Classroom Behavior", *The Journal of Educational Research* 65 (April 1972):365-368.

94. Thomas Samph, "Teacher Behavior and the Reading Performance of Below-Average Achievers," *The Journal of Educational Research* 67 (February 1974):268-270.

95. Sylvia P. McDaniel, "The Effects of Selected Teacher Personality Variables on Reading Readiness, Self-Concept and Changes in IQ in Culturally Deprived Five-Year-Olds", *Dissertation Abstracts*, 31 (Ann Arbor, Michigan: University Microfilms, a Xerox Company, 1970-1971), p. 6409-A.

96. Judith S. Bazemore, *The Relationship between Student Level of Tension, the Learning Environment and Achievement in Reading* (Bethesda, Md.: Eric Document Reproduction Service, ED 070 038, 1971).

97. Jeanne Chall and Shirley Feldman, "First Grade Reading: An Analysis of the Interaction of Professed Methods, Teacher Implementation and Child Backgrounds," *The Reading Teacher* 19 (May 1966):569-575.

98. Albert J. Harris, "The Effective Teacher of Reading", <u>The Reading Teacher</u> 23 (December 1969):195-204.

99. Mildred J. Prows, "An Attempt to Increase Reading Achievement by Organizing Instruction and Sensitizing the Teacher to Build Positive Self-Concepts", <u>Dissertation Abstracts,</u> 29 (Ann Arbor, Michigan: University Microfilms, a Xerox Company, 1967), pp. 187-A-188-A.

100. Glenn Heathers, "Grouping", in <u>Encyclopedia of Educational Research,</u> 4th ed. edited by: Robert L. Ebel (Toronto: The Macmillan Company, 1969), pp. 564-568.

101. Antoinette McChristey, "A Comparative Study to Determine Whether Self-Selection Reading Can Be Successfully Used at Second Grade Level" (Ed.M. thesis, University of Southern California, 1957).

102. Frances Cynog, "Self-Selection in Reading: Report of a Longitudinal Study", in <u>Reading and the Elementary School Child</u>, eds: Virgil M. Howes and Helen Fisher Darrow (New York: The Macmillan Company, 1968), pp. 203-236.

103. Ibid., p. 234.

104. Philip J. Acinapuro, "A Comparative Study of the Results of Two Reading Programs--An Individualized Pattern and a Three Group Pattern" (Ed.D. dissertation, Teachers College, Columbia University, 1959).

105. Rodney Johnson, "Individual and Basal Reading Programs", <u>Elementary English</u> 42 (December 1965):902-904,915.

106. Ibid., p. 904.

107. Anna E. Teigland, <u>An Experimental Study of Individualized and Basal Reader Approaches to Teaching Reading in Grades One and Two</u> (Bethesda, Md.: Eric Document Reproduction Service, ED 047 901, 1971).

108. Ben A. Bonhorst and Sophia Sellers, "Individualized Reading Vs. Textbook Instruction", <u>Elementary English</u> 36 (March 1959): 185-190.

109. Ibid., 190.

110. Claire Walker, "An Evaluation of Two Programs in Reading in Grades Four, Five and Six" (Ed.D. dissertation, New York University, 1957).

111. Ruth K. Izzo, "A Comparison of Two Teaching Methods, Individual and Group, in the Teaching of Word Identification in Beginning Reading" (Ed.D. dissertation, New York University, 1960).

112. Margaret Bradford, "A Comparison of Two Teaching Methods, Individualized and Group, in the Teaching of Comprehension in Beginning Reading" (Ed.D. dissertation, New York University, 1960).

113. Phyllis Adams, "An Investigation of an Individualized Reading Program and a Modified Basal Reading Program in First Grade" (Ed.D. dissertation, University of Denver, 1962).

114. Harry Sartain, "The Roseville Experiment with Individualized Reading", <u>The Reading Teacher</u> 13 (April 1960):277-281.

115. Ibid., p. 280.

116. Ibid., p. 281.

117. Harold Karr, "An Experiment with an Individualized Method of Teaching Reading". The Reading Teacher 18 (February 1967):174-177.

118. Irving H. Anderson et al., "The Relationship between Reading Achievement and the Method of Teaching Reading", University of Michigan School of Education Bulletin 38 (May 1961):320-327.

119. Alton L. Safford, "Evaluation of an Individualized Reading Program", The Reading Teacher 12 (April 1960):266-270.

120. Ibid., p. 270

121. Salvatore D. Marani, "The Effect of Methods of Teaching Reading on the Reading Achievement and Attitudes toward Self of Delinquent Boys", Dissertation Abstracts 32 (Ann Arbor, Michigan: University Microfilms, a Xerox Company, 1971), p. 4841-A.

122. James M. Marble, "An Analysis of the Effectiveness of Individualized Reading Instruction upon the Self-Concepts of Disadvantaged Students with Reading Disabilities", Dissertation Abstracts, 34 (Ann Arbor, Michigan: University Microfilms, a Xerox Company, 1974), p. 4571-A.

123. Norman E. Wallen and Robert M. W. Travers, "Analysis and Investigation of Teaching Methods", in Handbook of Research on Teaching, ed.: Nathaniel L. Gage (Chicago: Rand McNally and Company, 1963), pp. 470-478.

124. Ibid.

125. Roberta Weiner, "A Look at Reading Practices in the Open Classroom", The Reading Teacher 27 (February 1974):438-472.

126. Ibid., p. 472

127. Samuel Weintraub et al., review of Reading in Infant Classes, by E. J. Goodacre, in Reading Research Quarterly, 9, No. 3 1973-74, pp. 387-388.

128. Charles E. Silberman, Crisis in the Classroom (New York: Random House 1970), pp. 257-261; E. Kuno Beller, "Research on Organized Programs of Early Education", in Second Handbook of Research on Teaching, ed.: Robert M. W. Travers (Chicago: Rand McNally and Company, 1973), pp. 567-569; Nora L. Goddard, Reading in the Modern Infant School (London: University of London Press Ltd., 1969), pp. 6-7; Vera Southgate, "The Language Arts in Informal British Primary Classrooms", The Reading Teacher 26 (January 1973):367-373; and Weiner, "Reading Practices", pp. 438-442.

129. Children and Their Primary Schools, Vol. 1, p. 212, and Vol. 2 (Appendix 7), "cited by" Silberman, Crisis, p. 258.

130. Silberman, Crisis, p. 258.

131. Informal Versus Formal Education and Reading Attainment in the Junior School, quoted in Silberman, Crisis, pp. 259-260.

132. <u>Long Term Results of Infant School Methods</u>, "cited by" Southgate, "Language Arts", p. 371.

133. "Attainment and the School Environment","cited by" Southgate, Language Arts," p. 371.

134. Experiment and Tradition in Primary Schools, "cited by" Beller, "Research", pp. 567-568.

135. Beller, "Research", p. 568.

136. Laura D. Harckman, <u>The Effect of Informal and Formal British Infant Schools on Reading Achievement</u> (Bethesda, Md.: ERIC Document Reproduction Service, Ed 062 011, 1972).

137. Reading in the Primary School, "cited by" Southgate, "Language Arts", p. 371.

138. <u>The Roots of Reading,</u> "cited by" Southgate, Ibid.

139. <u>The Trend of Reading Standard</u>, "cited by" Weiner, "Reading Practices", p. 439.

140. Arthur W. Heilman, <u>Principles and Practices of Teaching Reading</u>, 3rd ed. (Columbus, Ohio: Charles E. Merrill Publishing Co., 1972), pp. 605-606.

141. Chester D. Harris, "The Psychology of Reading", <u>The Journal of Educational Research</u> 67 (May-June 1974):406.

142. Duker, "Needed Research in Individualized Reading", <u>Elementary English</u> 43 (March 1966):220-225; Gudelia A. Fox and Raymond B. Fox,"The Individualized Reading Controversy", <u>National Elementary School Principal</u> 44 (March 1965): 258-260; and Harry W. Sartain, "Individualized Reading: Conclusions Based on Research Reports", in <u>A Decade of Innovations,</u> ed.: Elaine Vilscek (Newark, Delaware: International Reading Association, 1967), pp. 64-72.

143. Heathers, "Grouping", p. 568.

CHAPTER III

THE DESIGN AND METHODOLOGY OF THE STUDY

The review of research in Chapter II describes implicitly and explicitly the issues and the problems which must be considered and dealt with in developing appropriate and useful methodological approaches and strategies for executing scientific research on the question of the relationships between classroom organization, self-concept and reading achievement. The thrust and trajectory of this research endeavor are contingent on and emerge from the work of previous researchers. This study is viewed as one contribution in addressing the broad question of self-concept, classroom organization and reading achievement. The purpose of this chapter is to provide a description of the research study and its constituent elements.

Purposes of the Study

The purposes of the study are as follows:

1. To investigate and describe the relationship between pre self-concept and reading readiness.

2. To investigate and describe the relationship between pre self-concept and reading achievement.

   2a. To investigate and describe the interaction effect of pre self-concept and classroom organization on reading achievement.

3. To investigate and describe the relationship between reading achievement and post self-concept.

4. To investigate and describe the difference between the post self-concept scores of children in the activity-centered classrooms and the post self-concept scores of children in the traditional classrooms.

   4a. To investigate and describe the differences between the post self-concept scores of children with high reading achievement scores and the post self-concept scores of children with low reading achievement scores.

   4b. To investigate and describe the interaction effect of classroom organization and reading achievement on post self-concept.

5. To investigate and describe the interaction effect of classroom organization and reading readiness on reading achievement.

   5a. To investigate and describe the differences between the reading achievement scores of children in the activity-centered classrooms and the reading achievement scores of children in the traditional classrooms.

   5b. To investigate and describe the differences between the reading achievement scores of those children who have high post self-concept scores and the reading achievement scores of those children who have low post self-concept scores.

5c. To investigate and describe the interaction effect of classroom organization and post self-concept on reading achievement.

Overview of the Design of the Study

Sample

Twelve first grade classrooms located in the states of New Hampshire or Maine were selected for this study. Of these classrooms six were organized according to traditional patterns and six were activity-centered.

All classrooms were located in school buildings which were designed according to traditional architectural configurations. The six activity-centered classrooms were housed in buildings in which both the traditional and activity-centered approaches to classroom organization were employed. Two of the traditional classrooms were housed in buildings in which only the traditional approach to organization was utilized. The remaining four of these classrooms were located in buildings in which both the traditional and activity-centered approaches were used.

Three activity-centered and three traditional classrooms were located in blue collar districts. Three activity-centered and three traditional classrooms were located in middle class districts.

Test Administration

The following tests were administered to the total sample of two hundred fifty-seven children:

1. a group reading readiness test

2. an individual self-concept test which measures the way the child sees himself, as well as the way he believes his mother, teacher, and peers see him

3. a group intelligence test

4. the reading subtests of a standardized achievement test

5. a post-test of the self-concept instrument

These tests are described in detail on pages 46-47.

Observational Data

Two informal observational visits and three formal observational visits were made by the investigator to each classroom. Teachers completed a personality instrument as well as an inventory of the types of materials which were either in their classroom or available to them in the school for purposes of reading instruction.

Analysis of Data

After all data were collected they were coded for statistical analysis. The quantifiable data were analyzed through: Pearson product-moment correlation; analysis of variance and analysis of co-variance; the descriptive data were summarized by the writer.

Preliminary Considerations

Classroom Structure

For purposes of this study the following definitions of classroom structure were adhered to:

<u>Traditional Classroom</u> - classroom in which the curriculum and the instructional program are determined and prescribed by the teacher to the degree that the children must adjust themselves to the curriculum and program. This classroom is more curriculum-oriented than child-centered.

<u>Activity-Centered Classroom</u> - classroom in which instruction is carefully geared to meet the individual needs and abilities of children; in which play is perceived as a valuable learning experience, which is more child and project centered than teacher dominated; in which the child has the freedom to pursue his own interests, make decisions, explore and discover within the parameters of a curriculum designed to meet his needs. This classroom is frequently referred to as informal and is modeled after the British Infant Schools.

Criteria for Teacher Selection

In comparing the effects of specific approaches to classroom organization, it is essential that those who utilize a specific approach share: 1) a common philosophical base; 2) a similar background of training, experience and understanding regarding the rationale for and techniques of implementing such an approach; and 3) a commitment to and belief in the value of the approach.

a) <u>The Activity-Centered Teachers</u>

Based on these criteria, the activity-centered teachers were selected from among the graduates of the Early Childhood Program at the University of New Hampshire. In this particular graduate program the students, who are experienced teachers, first engage in summer session seminars designed not only to increase their knowledge of child development but also to provide expertise in establishing and conducting a child-centered learning environment.

Next the students undertake an extensive, field-based practicum experience which spans a full academic year. The major responsibilities for this portion of the program are:

1. to plan, organize, staff and develop a model early learning center in a local school district.

2. to provide in-service experiences for teachers, administrators, volunteer parent aides, and senior students majoring in elementary education.

3. to write regularly for the monthly Early Childhood Newsletter, thus providing teacher development assistance through: sharing personal analyses and reflections upon teaching young children; publicizing information about significant events in early education; reporting reviews of Early Childhood research, as well as reviewing educational materials, books, journal articles and films.

4. to design and execute an Early Childhood Conference for teachers and administrators of the Northern New England area. In this instance the participants

do all the conference planning, present lecturers, panel discussions, films, video-tapes, slides, displays, book sales, publicity and programming.

In addition the graduate students pursue prescribed courses, participate in workshops on educational topics and areas of current interest, and prepare two independent studies during the academic year.

In summary participants in the Early Childhood Program learn by doing, with a major proportion of their time spent in field-based learning experiences. The program is structured in such a way that students are required to assume major responsibility in a local school district and to demonstrate initiatory, creative, problem solving and child-centered approaches in classroom organization and curriculum development.

b) The Traditional Classroom Teacher

These teachers were prepared through conventional teacher education programs with emphasized didactic, academic instruction through discrete structured courses with limited field-based experiences confined to one semester of student teaching. This practicum experience consisted of two major elements: 1) work under the guidance of a cooperating classroom teacher, and 2) supervision by a university or college faculty member. Supervisory visits in these preparatory programs ranged from four to six per semester. In all instances, the student was encouraged to model the classroom behavior of her cooperating teacher.

Further training for the traditional teachers consisted of in-service programs which focused primarily on methods and materials. These programs which were presented in the form of workshops were offered on an ad hoc basis and were not integrated into a cohesive training program. In addition, they did not support any particular approach or philosophy of education.

In summary both the activity-centered and the traditional teachers exemplified the practices of classroom organization which met the requirements of the definitions of the activity-centered and traditional classroom organization employed in this study.

Initiating the Study

Selecting the Classroom

This investigator held a faculty position at the University of New Hampshire as an instructor in the Early Childhood Program described above for four years prior to the initiation of this study. During that period of time her primary responsibilities were to function as a consultant to the students in their school settings and to assist them in their endeavors to establish, maintain and develop activity-centered classrooms which adhered to the philosophy of child-centered education. During that period of time she had many opportunities to observe and evaluate the professional behavior of several students.

In June of 1973, the investigator again visited the classrooms of those graduates of the program who were then teaching first grade to observe teacher behavior and ensure the fact that these former students were implementing the activity-centered philosophy. Those whom she judged to be performing with a high degree of excellence were asked to participate in this research endeavor. All six of the activity-centered teachers who were approached agreed to become involved in the study.

A different procedure was utilized to select the traditional teachers. In this instance, the investigator met with the principal and reading consultant of schools in which she had supervised undergraduate student teachers over the years. The principal and reading consultant were asked to:

1. identify first grade teachers who preferred the traditional approach to classroom organization, were committed to this philosophy, and who based on their judgments performed with a high degree of excellence.

2. complete an instrument designed by the investigator to assess the recommended teachers' classroom performance (Appendix, pp. 91).

The eleven teachers who were recommended and achieved an overall rating of above average or outstanding were further screened by the investigator on the basis of age and years of teaching experience in an attempt to match the teachers in each group on these criteria. Finally the six selected teachers were asked to participate in the study. All six of the traditional teachers who were approached agreed to become involved.

Specifically all twelve teachers agreed: 1) to complete a pre- and post-testing on The Adjective Check List;[144] 2) to complete a materials inventory; 3) to allow the investigator to visit in their classrooms throughout the year; and 4) to permit her to administer a number of tests to their first grade children.

The permission of the superintendent of schools was requested in all cases. Generally, this permission was swiftly granted. However, in two instances it was necessary to secure the permission of the school board as well as that of the parents of the children who were to be involved. In total ten schools in eight different communities were involved in the study.

Approximately two weeks before the commencement of the 1973-74 school year, the twelve teachers who had agreed to participate in the study were contacted by mail. At that time they were presented with a review of the investigator's plans and the initial testing schedule. Follow-up letters were also sent in November, February and April to announce the upcoming testing dates.

The Subjects of the Study

All pupils in the six activity-centered and six traditional classrooms were included in the study. The 133 activity-centered students ranged in age from 5 years, 9 months to 8 years, 1 month. In this group there were 69 boys and 64 girls. The 124 traditional group students had an age range of 5 years, 10 months to 8 years, 4 months. There was a total of 61 boys and 63 girls in these classrooms.

Selecting the Instruments

Reading readiness test - A test suitable for group administration was required to assess the reading readiness level of each incoming first grade student. The Murphy-Durrell Reading Readiness Analysis,[145] a research-based refinement of the Murphy-Durrell Reading Readiness Test, was selected for this purpose. In this test emphasis is placed on: teaching before testing in the administration of the phonemes subtest; dictation of letters by the teacher in the letter names subtest; the administration of the learning rate subtest in a group situation. The publishers report that the reliability of the instrument was assessed by the odd-even split-half method corrected by the Spearman-Brown Prophecy Formula. These statistical treatments yielded a coefficient of .98 for the total tests with the phonemes, letter names, and learning rate subtests yielding coefficients of .94, .99 and .88 respectively.[146]

Concurrent validity between the total score on the instrument and that of the Metropolitan Readiness Test was found to be .80. Predictive validity as demonstrated by correlations with end of the year administration of the Stanford Achievement Test - Primary I Reading Tests ranged from .65 to .66.[147]

Reading achievement test - The Metropolitan Achievement Tests[148] Primary I Reading subtests were selected to assess the end of the year reading achievement of the students in the sample. This instrument is the fourth edition of Metropolitan Achievement Tests,[149] a successor to the 1958 edition. Reliability for the total reading subtests as determined by the split-half (odd-even) method corrected by the Spearman-Brown Formula is reported as .96. Use of Saupe's estimate of Kuder-Richardson Formula 20 reliability yielded a coefficient of .97. The authors encourage prospective users of this instrument to inspect publisher-prepared content outlines to insure content validity of the instrument for their particular school system.[150]

Intelligence test - The Pintner-Cunningham Primary Test[151] was chosen to assess the intelligence quotient of the children. This test intended for kindergarten and grade one but useful also at the beginning of grade two is composed entirely of pictures which are marked by the children according to the examiner's verbal directions. It contains seven different subtests which according to the authors cover as many different aspects of mental ability. The authors believe that the best evidence of the validity of this instrument rests upon the satisfied experiences of those who have used it successfully over the years.[152] A correlation of scores obtained on this instrument with those on the Metropolitan Readiness Test yielded coefficients of .66, .65, .62, and .63. Moreover, coefficients of .77, .75, .73 and .76 were obtained when scores obtained on the Pintner-Cunningham Primary Test and the Murphy-Durrell Readiness Test were correlated.[153] A predictive validity correlation of .55 was also yielded when total reading scores obtained on the Metropolitan Achievement Test - Primary I were correlated with total scores obtained on the instrument.[154]

Self-Concept instrument - The investigator based her selection of The Thomas Self-Concept Values Test[155] on the findings of Coller who, after careful review of more than fifty currently available instruments which purport to assess the self-concept of the young child, included this test in his listing of those which have been or are presently being administered to large samples, under diverse conditioning.[156]

This instrument which measures the way the child sees himself, as well as the way he believes his teacher, mother and peers see him has a test-retest reliability coefficient of .78 for the total self-concept score.[157] The author suggests that the test has construct validity as determined by its format, logically selected item content and the independent scale scores.[158] Thomas also found low but significant correlational coefficients when various self-concept scores were compared to such demographic variables as: number of siblings, amount of father's education and the child's age.[159] The author also investigated the socio-economic status variable and found the scale able to differentiate between highly privileged and underprivileged groups.[160]

Teacher personality - Since the investigator wished to control the data for the variable of teacher personality, an instrument designed to assess adult personality was necessitated. The 300 word, self-administered Adjective Check List[161] was selected for this purpose. Test-retest reliability for this scale was obtained with a sample of 100 adult males. In this instance the reliability coefficients varied from .01 to .86 with a mean of .54.[162] To further assess the reliability of this scale, the authors had 10 observers complete the instrument on the 20th, 40th, 60th, 80th and 100th man in this sample of 100. The five inter-group reliability coefficients corrected by the Spearman-Brown Prophecy Formula were .70, .63, .61, .75, and .61 respectively.[163] The manual also contains reports of a number of validation studies for this instrument.[164]

<u>Classroom observation guide</u> - The Bank Street Follow Through, 1970 guide entitled "Your Classroom As You See It"[165] was selected by the investigator to guide classroom observations when she visited in both the activity-centered and traditional classrooms. When this check list is utilized, attention is focused on: the physical environment; materials and equipment; displays; classroom library, classroom management, movement from one activity to another; grouping arrangements; and classroom climate. No reliability or validity data are available on this informal instrument (Appendix pp. 92-96.)

<u>Inventory of materials</u> - In order to control for the possibility that the activity-centered classrooms might be more adequately equipped with commercially prepared reading materials, specific information was needed regarding the materials available to each teacher in each type of classroom. Therefore a questionnaire was designed by the investigator to solicit information in this area. Questions were also asked about the teacher's satisfaction with the materials available to her, and whether she found it necessary to supplement them with materials and approaches of her own (Appendix p.97.)

<u>Teacher evaluation instrument</u> - Since the investigator desired to control the criteria on which the principals and reading consultants recommended the traditional teachers, she designed an informal teacher evaluation instrument to be used by those involved in the selection process. This instrument focused on the areas of classroom atmosphere and classroom performance. Teachers were rated on a scale of one to five (unsatisfactory through outstanding) on subsets of these topics. No reliability or validity data are available on this informal instrument (Appendix, p. 91).

Data Collection

The collection of data was initiated one week after the opening of school and continued throughout the school year.

<u>Testing Schedule</u>

September 10-26

1. The Thomas Self-Concept Values Test[166] was individually administered by the investigator to the first grade children in the six traditional and six activity-centered classrooms. Since this test which measures how the child sees himself as well as how he believes his mother, teachers, and peers see him, requires that the child be photographed prior to the administration of the instrument, black and white polaroid shots were taken of each child.

Prior to the administration of the test the investigator also established rapport by talking briefly with the child about the boy or girl in the picture.

In most instances the children were relaxed, willing to cooperate and responsive. If however the examiner considered that a child felt insecure or ill-at-ease, testing was not pursued further.

Occasionally a child found it difficult to give a "yes" or "no" response to a specific question. In this instance the investigator encouraged the child to try to make a choice. If, however, he persisted in his ambivalence, the item was scored N (no response) as suggested in the test manual.

Pupils were not limited in the amount of time they were given to respond to the test item and as a result testing time varied somewhat. However, the average time spent was twelve minutes per child.

2. The Adjective Check List,[167] an adult personality assessment instrument, was completed by each teacher on the day of her children's initial testing.

September 27-October 12

1. The Murphy-Durrell Reading Readiness Analysis [168] was administered to all children in the sample during this period of time. To facilitate the administration of this group test, and assure the validity of the test scores, the classroom teacher was asked to assist the investigator while she administered the instrument to the total group of children.

November-December-January

1. Since the investigator was very aware of the emotional impact that the holiday season has on young children, she decided to spread the administration of the Pintner-Cunningham Primary Test[169] over a longer period of time, scheduling it in such a way as to avoid the weeks preceding holidays and vacations. As a result this intelligence test was given in four classrooms in November, four in December and four in January. In addition, the investigator found it necessary to schedule make-ups on this test during the month of February, because of the absentee rate at the time of the initial testing.

April 23-June 10

During this period of time, the investigator spent the major portion of two and one-half days in each classroom. Day one was spent in the post-test administration of The Thomas Self-Concept Values Test.[170] On the second day, the children were given the Word Knowledge and Word Analysis subtests of the Metropolitan Achievement Test. [171] The testing program concluded on the morning of the third day, with the children receiving the Reading subtest of this standardized instrument.

Classroom Observations and Materials Inventory

Classroom observations, to assure the fact that both groups of teachers were adhering to their organizational patterns, were conducted both formally and informally. In the latter instance, observations were undertaken as the investigator administered the self-concept test to individual children in the classroom setting. However three formal observations of approximately one hour's duration were undertaken in each of the classrooms from November to March. On these occasions, the investigator recorded her findings on the check list, "Your Classroom As You See It",[172] which has been described earlier.

On the first of these formal observational visits the teacher was asked to complete a materials inventory designed to solicit information regarding the materials available for purposes of teaching reading. This inventory was administered to control for the possibility that the activity-centered classrooms might be more adequately equipped with commercially prepared reading materials.

Anecdotal Data

The principals and teachers provided the investigator with ready access to the school records of each child. Thus, the following anecdotal data were collected on the two hundred fifty-seven children: date of birth; sex; number of children in the family; ordinal position among siblings; and previous school experience, i.e., kindergarten, readiness room, repetition of first grade.

Assumptions of the Study

1. It is assumed that the children's responses to the items on the self-concept test were accurate indications of their feelings.

2. It is assumed that achievement test data were collected under positive conditions and from receptive children.

3. It is assumed that there were no major disruptive events which affected the educational programs in either the activity-centered or traditional classrooms.

Limitations of the Study

1. This study is a quasi-experimental design limited to those classrooms which could be identified as activity-centered and traditional and which were available for this study. Therefore the limitations of this piece of research involve limitations of place and sampling.

2. The investigator was unable to control for all socio-economic variables. Controls were not available because the investigator had to work with classrooms which were available for research and which met the definitions of activity-centered and traditional classrooms.

3. Since it is generally accepted that self-concept changes slowly, a study of one year's duration may not have been sufficient for significant changes to manifest themselves.

4. This study was limited to first grade children who because of their limited school experience may not have encountered the quantity of successful or unsuccessful experience in reading necessary to affect the self-concept.

5. The findings of this study are limited to the validity of the measurement instruments used.

CHAPTER SUMMARY

Data for the study was collected from a sample of two hundred fifty-seven first grade children and twelve classroom teachers distributed among six activity-centered classrooms and six traditional classrooms. Data were collected through the use of standardized measuring instruments, observational check lists, and instructional and materials inventory, and informal observations. The quantifiable data were analyzed through: Pearson product-moment correlation, analysis of variance and analysis of covariance; the descriptive data were summarized by the writer. The results of these analyses are reported in Chapter IV.

Footnotes:

144. Harrison G. Gough and Alfred B. Heilburn, The Adjective Check List (Palo Alto, California: Consulting Psychologist Press, 1952).

145. Murphy and Durrell, The Murphy-Durrell Reading Readiness Analysis.

146. Helen A. Murphy and Donald D. Durrell, Murphy-Durrell Reading Readiness Analysis Manual of Directions (New York: Harcourt, Brace and World, Inc., 1965), p. 18.

147. Ibid., pp. 18-19.

148. Durost et al., Metropolitan Achievement Tests.

149. Walter N. Durost et al., Metropolitan Achievement Tests, Primary I Teacher's Handbook (New York: Harcourt Brace Javonovich, Inc., 1971), p. 14.

150. Ibid., pp. 13-14.

151. Pintner, Cunningham and Durost, Pintner-Cunningham Primary Test.

152. Rudolph Pintner, Bess V. Cunningham and Walter N. Durost, Pintner-Cunningham Primary Test Directions for Administering, Scoring and Interpreting (New York: Harcourt, Brace and World, Inc., 1966), p. 16.

153. Ibid., pp. 16-17.

154. Ibid., p. 17.

155. Walter L. Thomas, The Thomas Self-Concept Values Test, rev. ed. (Grand Rapids, Michigan: Educational Service Company, 1969).

156. Allan R. Coller, The Assessment of Self-Concept in Early Childhood Education (Urbana, Illinois: University of Illinois, Eric Clearing House on Early Childhood Education, 1971), p. 45.

157. Thomas, The Thomas Self-Concept Values Test, pp. 31-32.

158. Ibid., pp. 33-34.

159. Ibid., pp. 37-38.

160. Coller, The Assessment of Self-Concept, p. 37.

161. Gough and Heilburn, The Adjective Check List.

162. Harrison G. Gough and Alfred B. Heilburn, The Adjective Check List Manual (Palo Alto, California: Consulting Psychologists Press, 1965), pp. 12-13.

163. Ibid., p. 13.

164. Ibid., pp. 14-16.

165. Bank Street Follow Through, "Your Classroom As You See It", New York, 1970. (Mimeographed.)

166. Thomas, *The Thomas Self-Concept Values Test*.

167. Gough and Heilburn, *The Adjective Check List*.

168. Murphy and Durrell, *Murphy-Durrell Reading Readiness Analysis*.

169. Pintner, Cunningham and Durost, *Pintner-Cunningham Primary Test*.

170. Thomas, *The Thomas Self-Concept Values Test*.

171. Durost et al., *Metropolitan Achievement Tests*.

172. Bank Street Follow Through, "Your Children As You See It."

CHAPTER IV

ANALYSIS OF THE DATA

In Chapter III the methodology of this study, which investigated the relationships between self-concept, classroom organization and reading achievement, was discussed. Chapter IV presents the analysis of the data yielded.

In summarizing the data a description of the sample is given together with the results of the statistical tests applied in securing answers to the following questions and sub-questions:

1. What is the relationship between pre self-concept and reading readiness?

2. What is the relationship between pre self-concept and reading achievement?

    2a. What is the interaction effect of pre self-concept and classroom organization on reading achievement?

3. What is the relationship between reading achievement and post self-concept?

4. Will there be a difference between the post self-concept scores of children in the activity-centered classrooms and the post self-concept scores of children in the traditional classrooms?

    4a. Will there be a difference between the post self-concept scores of children with high reading achievement scores and the post self-concept scores of children with low reading achievement scores?

    4b. What is the interaction effect of classroom organization and reading achievement on post self-concept?

5. What is the interaction effect of classroom organization and reading readiness on reading achievement?

    5a. Will there be a difference between the reading achievement scores of children in the activity-centered classrooms and the reading achievement scores of children in the traditional classrooms?

    5b. Will there be a difference between the reading achievement scores of those children who have high post self-concept scores and the reading achievement scores of those children who have low post self-concept scores?

    5c. What is the interaction effect of classroom organization and post self-concept on reading achievement?

In addition the data which describes 1) teacher personality; 2) the results of classroom observations; and 3) the availability of materials for reading instruction in each type of classroom as well as the teachers' satisfaction with these materials are summarized. Finally examples of the approaches which were employed to adjust instruction in each type of classroom are presented.

Description of the Sample

Twelve first grade classrooms located in the states of New Hampshire or Maine were selected for this study. Of the twelve classrooms six were organized according to traditional patterns, while the remaining six were activity centered. Initially 284 children were involved in the study. Because of absenteeism or the invalid test results of a small number of children the sample was reduced to 257. Of this number, 124 children were in the traditional classrooms and 133 children were in the activity-centered classrooms.

Chronological Age

The variable of age was analyzed by a simple analysis of variance. The results of this analysis indicated that there was no significant difference between groups on this variable.

Table 1 reports the summary of the analysis of variance.

TABLE 1

MEAN CHRONOLOGICAL AGE OF CHILDREN IN THE ACTIVITY-CENTERED AND TRADITIONAL CLASSROOMS, STANDARD DEVIATIONS AND F RATIOS

	Activity-Centered Classrooms (N=133)		Traditional Classrooms (N=124)		
	Mean	Standard Deviation	Mean	Standard Deviation	F ratio
Chronological Age	78.57 months	5.39	78.82 months	5.36	.14
	df=1,255				

Sex

There was a total of 257 children in the sample. Of this number 127 were boys and 130 were girls.

Table 2 reports the total number of boys and girls in each type of classroom.

TABLE 2

DISTRIBUTION OF BOYS AND GIRLS IN THE ACTIVITY-CENTERED AND TRADITIONAL CLASSROOMS

	Activity-Centered Classrooms (N=133)	Traditional Classrooms (N=124)
Boys	66	61
Girls.	67	63
Total.	133	124

IQ

The Pintner-Cunningham Primary Test[173] was administered to the total sample in order to determine the mean IQ score for each group. The data were analyzed by a simple analysis of variance. The results of this analysis indicated that there was no significant difference between groups in mean IQ score.

Table 3 reports the summary of the analysis of variance.

TABLE 3

MEAN IQ SCORES OF CHILDREN IN THE ACTIVITY-CENTERED AND TRADITIONAL CLASSROOMS, STANDARD DEVIATIONS AND F RATIOS

	Activity-Centered Classrooms (N=133)		Traditional Classrooms (N=124)		
	Mean	Standard Deviation	Mean	Standard Deviation	F ratio
IQ	107.872	18.18	108.69	16.72	.14

Pre Self-Concept

The Thomas Self-Concept Values Test[174] was administered to the total sample during the month of September in order to determine the mean pre self-concept scores for the activity-centered group and the traditional group. The data were analyzed by a simple analysis of variance. The results of this analysis indicated that there was no significant difference between groups on any of the self-concept subtest mean scores or on the total self-concept mean score. Of our four subtests, the mean self-as-subject score of the activity-centered group approached significance.[175]

Table 4 reports the summary of the analysis of variance.

TABLE 4

MEAN PRE SELF-CONCEPT SCORES OF CHILDREN IN THE ACTIVITY-CENTERED AND TRADITIONAL CLASSROOMS, STANDARD DEVIATIONS AND F RATIOS

Pre Self-Concept	Activity-Centered Classrooms (N=133)		Traditional Classrooms (N=124)		
	Mean	Standard Deviation	Mean	Standard Deviation	F ratio
Self-as-Subject	7.59	3.44	6.77	3.48	3.58
Mother Referent	7.45	3.44	6.93	3.43	1.57
Teacher Referent	7.79	3.37	7.44	3.10	.76
Peer Referent	7.75	3.60	6.98	3.65	2.92
Total Self-Concept	30.09	13.56	28.04	12.31	1.59

df=1,225

Reading Readiness

The Murphy-Durrell Reading Readiness Analysis[176] was administered to the total sample during the latter part of September and the first two weeks of October in order to determine the mean reading readiness score for each group. The data were analyzed by a simple analysis of variance. The results of this analysis indicated that there was no significant difference between groups on the reading readiness subtests. These data also indicated that there was no significant difference between groups on the total test scores.

Table 5 reports the summary of the analysis of variance.

TABLE 5

MEAN READING READINESS SCORES OF CHILDREN IN THE
ACTIVITY-CENTERED AND TRADITIONAL CLASSROOMS,
STANDARD DEVIATIONS AND F RATIOS

Reading Readiness	Activity-Centered Classrooms (N=133)		Traditional Classrooms (N=124)		F ratio
	Mean	Standard Deviation	Mean	Standard Deviation	
Phonemes	42.04	8.56	42.87	6.33	.77
Letter Names	46.68	7.41	47.50	6.01	.94
Learning Rate	13.90	3.90	13.48	4.46	.64
Total Test	102.44	17.72	103.92	14.65	.52

df=1,255

In summary, the randomness of the sampling resulted in a matched grouping of children in the activity-centered and traditional classrooms. There was no significant differences between the groups in age, sex, intelligence, reading readiness and pre self-concept.

Research Questions

This section of the chapter presents a summary of the results of the statistical tests applied in securing answers to the questions of this study.

In obtaining the data needed to answer these questions The Thomas Self-Concept Values Test was administered at the beginning of first grade yielding a pre self-concept score. Reading readiness was determined by the scores obtained by the administration of The Murphy-Durrell Reading Readiness Analysis at the beginning of the school year. The reading subtests of the Metropolitan Achievement Tests[177] were given at the end of the school year yielding a reading achievement score. A post test administration of The Thomas Self-Concept Values Test was completed at the end of the school year, thus providing the investigator with post self-concept scores.

The quantifiable data were analyzed through Pearson product-moment correlation, analysis of variance and analysis of covariance. Garrett's table "F-ratios for .05 and .01 levels of significance" was used to determine significance between means.[178] The results are reported below.

1. What is the relationship between pre self-concept and reading readiness?

TABLE 6

INTERCORRELATION MATRIX OF ALL VARIABLES

	Word Knowledge	Word Analysis	Reading	Total Reading	Phonemes	Letter Names	Learning Rate	Total Test	IQ	Pre Self	Pre Mother	Pre Teacher	Pre Peer	Pre Total	Post Self	Post Mother	Post Teacher	Post Peer	Post Total
Word Knowledge	0	.89	.77	.91	.68	.68	.64	.76	.49	-.04	-.06	-.08	-.01	-.09	.00	-.03	.01	-.05	-.00
Word Analysis		0	.74	.84	.69	.65	.70	.75	.48	-.05	-.05	-.06	-.07	-.08	.04	-.03	.03	-.04	-.01
Reading			0	.96	.58	.49	.63	.63	.46	-.05	-.08	-.09	-.12	-.12	-.08	-.08	-.01	-.04	-.05
Total Reading				0	.66	.61	.67	.73	.50	-.06	-.08	-.10	-.12	-.12	-.05	-.06	-.01	-.05	-.04
Phonemes					0	.71	.64	.92	.42	-.11	-.10	-.14	-.17	-.16	-.04	-.10	-.06	-.08	-.07
Letter Names						0	.58	.89	.41	-.09	-.10	-.11	-.11	-.12	-.07	-.07	-.06	-.15	-.08
Learning Rate							0	.80	.35	-.11	-.11	-.12	-.09	-.13	-.04	-.02	-.01	.03	.01
Total Test								0	.45	-.12	-.11	-.14	-.14	-.15	-.05	-.07	-.05	-.09	-.06
IQ									0	-.04	-.04	-.04	.00	-.05	-.06	-.04	-.00	-.02	-.02
Pre Self										0	.77	.74	.73	.88	.46	.43	.45	.36	.47
Pre Mother											0	.78	.74	.88	.42	.44	.37	.37	.44
Pre Teacher												0	.81	.88	.43	.42	.45	.39	.46
Pre Peer													0	.87	.46	.52	.50	.44	.54
Pre Total														0	.48	.47	.47	.43	.51
Post Self															0	.76	.73	.69	.88
Post Mother																0	.81	.72	.92
Post Teacher																	0	.74	.92
Post Peer																		0	.85
Post Total																			0

N=257

Correlations were run on all variables in the study. An analysis of the resultant intercorrelation matrix (Table 6) indicates that there were no significant correlations between any of the subtests of The Thomas Self-Concept Values Test or the pre total self-concept scores and any of the subtests of The Murphy-Durrell Reading Readiness Analysis or the total reading readiness score.

Table 7 presents these data more concisely.

TABLE 7

CORRELATIONS BETWEEN PRE SELF-CONCEPT AND READING READINESS

Pre Self-Concept	Reading Readiness			
	Phonemes	Letter Names	Learning Rate	Total Test
Self-as-Subject	-.11	-.09	-.11	-.12
Mother Referent	-.10	-.11	-.11	-.11
Teacher Referent	-.14	-.11	-.12	-.14
Peer Referent	-.17	-.12	-.09	-.14
Total Self-Concept	-.16	-.07	-.13	-.15

N=257

It was concluded that there was no relationship between pre self-concept and reading readiness.

2. What is the relationship between pre self-concept and reading achievement?

An analysis of the intercorrelation matrix (Table 6) indicates that there were no significant correlations between any of the subtests of The Thomas Self-Concept Values Test or the pre total self-concept score and any of the reading subtests of the Metropolitan Achievement Test or the total reading score.

Table 8 presents these data.

TABLE 8

CORRELATIONS BETWEEN PRE SELF-CONCEPT AND READING ACHIEVEMENT

Pre Self-Concept	Reading Achievement			
	Word Knowledge	Word Analysis	Reading	Total Reading
Self-as Subject	-.04	-.05	-.05	-.06
Mother Referent	-.06	-.05	-.09	-.08
Teacher Referent	-.08	-.06	-.09	-.10
Peer Referent	-.01	-.07	-.12	-.12
Total Self-Concept	-.09	-.08	-.12	-.12

N=257

It was concluded that there was no relationship between pre self-concept and reading achievement.

2a. What is the interaction effect of pre self-concept and classroom organization on reading achievement?

Children in the activity-centered and traditional classrooms were divided into two groups on the basis of their pre self-concept scores. The high pre self-concept group consisted of those children who scored in the top half of <u>The Thomas Self-Concept Values Test</u> and the low pre self-concept group consisted of those children who scored on the bottom half of this test. On this basis the children in the sample were assigned to four groups: 1) activity-centered - high pre self-concept with an N of 68; 2) activity-centered - low pre self-concept with an N of 65; 3) traditional - high pre self-concept with an N of 61; and 4) traditional - low pre self-concept with an N of 63.

The data were analyzed by an analysis of covariance with self-concept scores and classroom organization as the independent variables; reading achievement as the dependent variable, and reading readiness as the covariate. The overall multivariate test was statistically significant (F=116.9938, P .0001). Univariate F tests for each independent variable and their interaction was conducted.

Table 9 reports the observed and adjusted mean reading achievement scores which indicated that the activity-centered classrooms have the higher adjusted mean score in reading achievement.

TABLE 9

OBSERVED AND ADJUSTED READING
ACHIEVEMENT MEAN SCORES

	Observed Means	Adjusted Means
Activity-Centered	57.39	57.80
Traditional	56.32	55.81
High Pre Self-Concept	66.29	58.49
Low Pre Self-Concept	47.40	55.11
Act-Cent/High Pre Self Concept	67.71	60.12
Act-Cent/Low Pre Self-Concept	46.60	55.48
Trad/High Pre Self-Concept	64.72	56.87
Trad/Low Pre Self-Concept	48.19	54.75

Table 10 presents the univariate analysis of the independent variables. There were no statistically significant main effects or interaction effects.

TABLE 10

UNIVARIATE ANALYSIS OF CLASSROOM ORGANIZATION
AND PRE SELF-CONCEPT ON READING ACHIEVEMENT

	M.S.	F	df	P
Classroom Organization	270.37	2.07	1,252	.1507
Pre Self-Concept	374.47	2.87	1,252	.0910
Classroom Organization X Pre Self-Concept	101.84	.782	1,252	.3772

It was concluded that there was no significant interaction effect of classroom organization and pre self-concept on reading achievement.

3. What is the relationship between reading achievement and post self-concept?

An analysis of the intercorrelation matrix (see Table 6) indicates that there were no significant relationships between any of the subtests of <u>The Thomas</u>

Self-Concept Values Test or the post total self-concept score and any of the subtests of the Metropolitan Achievement Test or the total reading score.

Table 11 presents these data.

TABLE 11

CORRELATIONS BETWEEN READING ACHIEVEMENT
AND POST SELF-CONCEPT

Reading Achievement	Post Self-Concept				
	Self-as-Subject	Mother Referent	Teacher Referent	Peer Referent	Total Self-Concept
Word Knowledge	.00	-.03	.01	-.05	-.00
Word Analysis	.04	-.03	.03	-.04	.01
Reading	-.08	-.08	-.01	-.04	-.05
Total Reading	-.05	-.06	-.01	-.05	-.04

N=257

It was concluded that there was no relationship between reading achievement and post self-concept.

4. Will there be a difference between the post self-concept scores of children in the activity-centered classrooms and the post self-concept scores of children in the traditional classrooms?

To answer this question The Thomas Self-Concept Values Test was readministered to the total sample at the end of the school year. The data were analyzed by a simple analysis of variance. The results of this analysis indicated that the children in the activity-centered classrooms achieved a mean score on the self-as-subject subtest of 7.91 while the children in the traditional classrooms obtained a mean score of 7.11. The analysis of variance test revealed statistical significance (F=4.48).

The mean score obtained by the children in the activity-centered classrooms on the mother referent subtest was 8.02 while the mean score obtained by the children in the traditional classrooms was 7.02. The analysis of variance test revealed statistical significance (F=5.63).

On the teacher referent subtest the mean score for the activity-centered classrooms on the mother referent subtest was 8.02 while the mean score obtained by the children in the traditional classrooms was 7.02. The analysis of variance test revealed statistical significance (F=5.63).

On the teacher referent subtest the mean score for the activity-centered children was 8.05 and the mean score for the activity-centered children was 8.05 and the mean score for the traditional children was 7.31. Although the difference between groups was not significant for this subtest, the F ratio (F=3.35) suggests that the difference approached significance.

The mean score obtained by the children in the activity-centered classrooms on the peer referent subtest was 7.98 while the mean score obtained by the children in the traditional classrooms was 7.10. Although the difference between groups was not significant for this subtest, the F ratio (F=3.62) suggests that the difference approached significance.

The mean total self-concept score obtained by the activity-centered children was 31.88, while the mean total self-concept score obtained by the traditional children was 28.44. The analysis of variance test revealed statistical significance (F=5.35).

Table 12 reports the mean post self-concept scores of both groups of children.

TABLE 12

MEAN POST SELF-CONCEPT SCORES OF CHILDREN IN THE
ACTIVITY-CENTERED AND TRADITIONAL CLASSROOMS,
STANDARD DEVIATIONS AND F RATIOS

Post Self-Concept	Activity-Centered Classrooms (N=133)		Traditional Classrooms (N=124)		
	Mean	Standard Deviation	Mean	Standard Deviation	F ratio
Self-as-Subject	7.91	3.02	7.11	3.11	4.48**
Mother Referent	8.02	3.16	7.02	3.61	5.63**
Teacher Referent	8.05	3.14	7.31	3.23	3.35
Peer Referent	7.98	3.81	7.10	3.56	3.62
Total Self-Concept	31.88	11.58	28.44	12.20	5.35**

**Statistically significant at .05 level.

It was found that there was a statistically significant difference between the total post self-concept scores of children in the activity-centered classrooms and the total self-concept scores of children in the traditional classrooms at the .05 level. The children in the activity-centered classrooms obtained the higher mean score.

4a. Will there be a difference between the post self-concept scores of children with high reading achievement scores and the post self-concept scores of children with low reading achievement scores?

4b. What is the interaction effect of classroom organization and reading achievement on post self-concept?

To answer these questions children in the activity-centered and traditional classrooms were divided into two groups on the basis of their reading achievement scores. The high reading achievement group consisted of those children who scored in the top half (at or above the fiftieth percentile) of the Metropolitan Achievement Test - Total Reading Score, and the low reading achievement group consisted of those children who scored in the bottom half (below the fiftieth percentile) of the same test. On this basis the children in the sample were assigned to four groups; activity-centered - high reading achievement with an N of 71; activity-centered low - reading achievement with an N of 62; traditional - high reading achievement with an N of 58; and traditional - low reading achievement with an N of 66. Mean post self-concept scores were computed for each of the four groups.

The data were analyzed by an analysis of covariance with classroom organization and reading achievement as the independent variables, post self-concept as the dependent variable, and pre self-concept as the covariate. The overall multivariate analysis test revealed statistical significance (F=86.21, P<.001). Univariate analyses of variance were conducted for each independent variable and their interaction. The results of the univariate analyses indicate that classroom organization has a significant effect on self-concept (F=3.78, P = .05) as related to year end reading achievement scores and that there is a significant interaction of classroom organization and reading achievement on self-concept (F=4.97, P = .0266). There is no significant effect of reading achievement on self-concept.

Table 13 reports the adjusted mean self-concept scores which indicated that the activity-centered classrooms have the greatest positive effect on self-concept as reflected in the highest adjusted mean post self-concept score.

Table 14 presents the univariate analyses of the independent variables.

TABLE 13

OBSERVED AND ADJUSTED POST SELF-CONCEPT MEAN SCORES

	Observed Means	Adjusted Means
Activity-Centered	31.88	31.28
Traditional	28.44	28.82
High Reading Achievement	29.82	30.28
Low Reading Achievement	30.62	29.83
Activity-Centered/High Reading Ach	32.83	32.94
Activity-Centered/Low Reading Ach	30.79	29.63
Traditional/High Reading Ach	26.14	27.62
Traditional/Low Reading Ach	30.45	30.03

TABLE 14

UNIVARIATE ANALYSIS OF CLASSROOM ORGANIZATION AND READING ACHIEVEMENT ON POST SELF-CONCEPT

	M.S.	F	df	P
Classroom Organization	397.59	3.78	1,252	.05**
Reading Achievement	19.19	0.18	1,252	.67
Classroom Organization X Reading Achievement	523.58	4.97	1,252	.02**

It was concluded that there is a statistically significant interaction effect of classroom organization and reading achievement on self-concept.

It was concluded that there was no main effect of reading achievement on self-concept.

It was concluded that classroom organization significantly affects self-concept. The data favored the activity-centered classroom.

5. What is the interaction effect of classroom organization and reading readiness on reading achievement?

To answer this question the children on the activity-centered and traditional classrooms were divided into two groups on the basis of their reading readiness scores. The high reading readiness group consisted of those children who scored in the top half (at or above the fiftieth percentile) of The Murphy-Durrell Reading Readiness Analysis and the low reading readiness group consisted of those children who scored in the bottom half (below the fiftieth percentile) of the same test which was administered at the beginning of the school year. On this basis the children in the sample were assigned to four groups: (1) activity-centered - high reading readiness with an N of 59; (2) activity-centered - low reading readiness with an N of 69; and (4) traditional - low reading readiness with an N of 55.

Table 15 reports the mean reading achievement test scores for each of the sample subgroups.

TABLE 15

MEAN READING ACHIEVEMENT TEST SCORES BY CLASSROOM ORGANIZATION, READING READINESS, AND CLASSROOM ORGANIZATION X READING READINESS

Group	Mean	N
Activity-Centered	57.39	133
Traditional	56.32	124
High Reading Readiness	59.73	128
Low Reading Readiness	54.04	129
Activity-Centered/High Reading Readiness	61.25	59
Activity-Centered/Low Reading Readiness	54.31	74
Traditional/High Reading Readiness	58.43	69
Traditional/Low Reading Readiness	53.67	25
Total Sample	56.92	257

The data were analyzed by a 4 way analysis of variance with classroom organization and reading readiness scores as the independent variables and reading achievement scores as the dependent variables. The results of the analysis indicated that the only variable affecting reading achievement at a statistically significant level was reading readiness (F=7.957, P = .0052). The variable of classroom organization and interaction of classroom organization X reading readiness were not statistically significant.

Table 16 reports the summary of the analysis of variance.

TABLE 16

SUMMARY TABLE - 4 WAY ANALYSIS OF VARIANCE: CLASSROOM ORGANIZATION, READING READINESS, AND READING ACHIEVEMENT

	S.S.	df	M.S.	F	P
Classroom Organization	189.343	1	189.343	0.694	.4055
High-Low Reading Readiness	2170.166	1	2170.166	7.957	.0052**
Classroom Organization X High-Low Reading Readiness	75.366	1	75.366	0.276	.5996
Error Between	69006.103	253	272.251		
Total	71440.978	256			

It was concluded that there was no interaction effect of classroom organization and reading readiness on reading achievement. The variable of reading readiness was found to have a statistically significant main effect at the .005 level on reading achievement. Classroom organization did not affect reading achievement at a statistically significant level.

    5a. Will there be a difference between the reading achievement scores of children in the activity-centered classrooms and the reading achievement scores of children in the traditional classrooms?

To answer this question, the reading subtests of the Metropolitan Achievement Test were administered to the total sample population. The data were analyzed by a simple analysis of variance. The results of this analysis indicated that children in the activity-centered classrooms achieved a mean score on the word knowledge subtest of 28.62, while the children in the traditional classrooms achieved a mean score of 28.75. On the word analysis subtest the activity-centered children obtained a mean score of 32.84 and the traditional children obtained a mean score of 32.67. On the reading subtest the children in the activity-centered classrooms obtained a mean score of 29.13 and the children in the traditional classrooms obtained a mean score of 27.65. The mean total reading score for the children in the activity-centered classrooms was 57.39 while the mean total reading score for the children in the traditional classrooms was 56.32. The difference between groups was not significant for either the reading subtests or the total reading score.

Table 17 reports the mean reading achievement scores of both groups of children.

TABLE 17

MEAN READING ACHIEVEMENT SCORES BY
CLASSROOM ORGANIZATION, STANDARD
DEVIATION AND F RATIO

Reading Achievement	Activity-Centered Classrooms (N=133)		Traditional Classrooms (N=124)		F ratio
	Mean	Standard Deviation	Mean	Standard Deviation	
Word Knowledge	28.62	7.91	28.74	6.19	.02
Word Analysis	32.84	8.60	32.67	7.23	.32
Reading	29.13	10.48	27.65	10.19	1.31
Total Reading	57.39	17.67	56.32	15.48	.26

df=1,255

It was concluded that there was no significant difference between the observed total reading achievement scores of children in the activity-centered classrooms and the observed total reading achievement scores of children in the traditional classrooms.

    5b. Will there be a difference between the reading achievement scores of those children who have high post self-concept scores and those children who have low post self-concept scores?

    5c. What is the interaction effect of classroom organization and post self-concept on reading achievement?

To answer these questions children in the activity-centered and traditional classrooms were divided into two groups on the basis of their post self-concept scores. Those children who scored in the top half (at or above the fiftieth percentile) of The Thomas Self-Concept Values Test were assigned to the high self-concept group. The low self-concept group consisted of those children who scored in the bottom half (below the fiftieth percentile) of this test. From these two groups children in the sample were assigned to four groups: (1) activity-centered - high post self-concept with an N of 74; (2) activity-centered low post self-concept with an N of 59; (3) traditional - high post self-concept with an N of 55; and (4) traditional - low post self-concept with an N of 69. The data were analyzed by an analysis of covariance with post self-concept scores and classroom organization as the independent variables and reading achievement as the dependent variable, with reading readiness as the covariate. The overall multivariate analysis test was statistically significant ($F=284.90$, $P<.001$).

Table 18 presents the observed and adjusted reading achievement means for each group.

TABLE 18

OBSERVED AND ADJUSTED READING
ACHIEVEMENT MEAN SCORES

	Observed Means	Adjusted Means
Activity-Centered	57.39	57.81
Traditional	56.32	55.52
High Post Self-Concept	55.37	56.08
Low Post Self-Concept	58.39	57.24
Activity-Centered/High Post Self-Concept	57.46	58.45
Activity-Centered/Low Post Self-Concept	57.31	57.17
Traditional/High Post Self-Concept	52.56	53.72
Traditional/Low Post Self-Concept	59.32	57.32

Univariate F tests for the independent variables and their interaction were conducted. Table 19 presents the univariate analysis of the independent variables. There were no statistically significant main effects or interaction effects.

TABLE 19

UNIVARIATE ANALYSIS OF CLASSROOM ORGANIZATION
AND POST SELF-CONCEPT ON READING
ACHIEVEMENT

	M.S.	F	df	P
Classroom Organization	298.88	2.30	1,252	.1310
Post Self-Concept	72.78	.56	1,252	.4554
Classroom Organization X Post Self-Concept	375.84	2.89	1,252	.0905

The interaction of classroom organization and post self-concept while not significant at the .05 level had a strong effect on reading achievement with a $P = .09$ with the activity-centered - high post self-concept group showing the highest adjusted mean score.

The variable of classroom organization while not significant at the .05 level had a strong effect with a $P = .13$ favoring the activity-centered classroom which showed the higher adjusted mean score of 57.81 over the traditional classroom adjusted mean score of 55.52.

It was concluded that there was no significant difference in the reading achievement scores of those children who have high post self-concept scores and those children who have low post self-concept scores.

It was further concluded that there is no significant interaction effect of classroom organization and post self-concept on reading achievement.

While there were no statistically significant main effects or interaction effect, it was found that the interaction of classroom organization and post self-concept had a strong effect with a P = .09 favoring the activity-centered high post self-concept group which showed the highest adjusted mean score.

Classroom organization was also found to have a strong effect with a P = .13 favoring the activity-centered classrooms which showed an adjusted mean score of 57.81 as compared to the adjusted mean score of 55.52 for the traditional classrooms.

Descriptive Data

Pre Personality of Teachers

The Adjective Check List[179] was used to obtain a personality profile of each of the teachers in the activity-centered classrooms and the traditional classrooms. This check list was administered at the beginning of the school year to the twelve teachers involved in the study. Raw scores were computed for the twenty-four scales of the check list for each teacher. The raw scores were then converted into standard scores. An arithmetic mean standard score for the activity-centered teachers and an arithmetic mean standard score for the traditional teachers were obtained for each of the twenty-four scales.

Table 20 presents the standard scores on each scale for every teacher in the study and the arithmetic mean standard score for the activity-centered and traditional teachers.

Using the arithmetic means, personality profiles for the activity-centered teachers and for the traditional teachers were plotted. Figure 1 shows the profiles on the pre Adjective Check List scales. The profiles for both groups of teachers were very similar with the greater differences appearing on the scales of achievement and endurance.

On the achievement scale the activity-centered teachers obtained a mean standard score of 59 as compared with a score of 48.83 for the traditional teachers. The range of scores for the activity-centered teachers was 50-63 as compared with the 29-74 range for the traditional teachers (Table 20). These data indicate that the activity-centered teachers were more homogeneous than the traditional teachers in the achievement scale.

According to the manual for The Adjective Check List the high scoring subject on achievement:

> .....is usually seen as intelligent and hard-working, but also as involved in his intellectual and other endeavors. He is

TABLE 20

PRE ADJECTIVE CHECK LIST STANDARD SCORES AND MEANS

Traditional Teachers

	A	B	C	D	E	F	Mn.
Number of Adjectives Checked	65	41	51	43	46	54	50.
Defensiveness	51	51	44	49	28	52	45.83
Number of Favorable Adjectives Checked	50	56	47	46	29	48	46.
Number of Unfavorable Adjectives Checked	39	40	64	65	68	37	52.17
Self-confidence	62	38	64	70	43	44	53.5
Self-control	51	53	46	43	32	61	47.66
Lability	65	45	45	68	51	53	54.5
Personal Adjustment	51	59	41	44	34	52	46.83
Achievement	59	29	58	74	33	40	48.83
Dominance	56	45	67	77	42	40	54.5
Endurance	49	52	58	60	32	45	42.5
Order	45	60	53	47	34	50	48.16
Intraception	61	58	42	53	16	42	45.33
Nurturance	55	62	32	44	29	57	46.5
Affiliation	62	51	51	39	34	54	48.5
Heterosexuality	49	52	48	56	37	42	47.33
Exhibition	58	42	63	58	54	32	51.16
Autonomy	46	38	74	59	52	47	52.66
Aggression	51	42	78	62	68	42	57.16
Chance	56	45	59	55	48	52	52.5
Succorance	47	49	42	33	53	51	45.83
Absement	48	57	26	27	50	52	43.33
Deference	49	61	27	23	52	56	44.66
Counseling Readiness	37	42	69	72	49	40	51.5

Activity-Centered Teachers

	A	B	C	D	E	F	Mn.
Number of Adjectives Checked	47	54	65	39	52	60	52.83
Defensiveness	49	62	55	55	43	47	52.
Number of Favorable Adjectives Checked	59	63	59	49	52	40	54.66
Number of Unfavorable Adjectives Checked	42	39	46	45	64	60	49.33
Self-confidence	55	68	76	46	51	48	54.
Self-control	51	59	42	49	42	57	51.33
Lability	54	43	62	59	68	45	52.83
Personal Adjustment	48	54	59	53	44	45	51.83
Achievement	58	62	63	57	50	63	59.
Dominance	64	60	68	53	54	62	59.33

Table 20 (Continued)

	Activity-Centered Teachers						
	A	B	C	D	E	F	Mn.
Endurance	50	59	60	59	44	46	54.
Order	49	54	54	51	45	43	53.
Intraception	39	62	60	58	51	42	52.16
Nurturance	54	62	55	62	47	45	53.83
Affiliation	55	59	50	62	41	55	53.83
Heterosexuality	54	57	61	53	42	55	51.5
Exhibition	54	59	72	50	51	61	54.5
Autonomy	52	55	63	45	50	53	53.
Aggression	46	52	59	59	56	69	56.5
Change	59	58	59	38	45	59	41.16
Succorance	44	39	22	52	53	53	47.83
Abasement	40	41	23	54	50	39	44.33
Deference	43	49	30	61	41	45	46.16
Counseling Readiness	39	37	45	51	49	51	44.83

FIGURE 1
PROFILE SHEET FOR THE ADJECTIVE CHECK LIST
PRE PERSONALITY PROFILE

Name_____ Age_____ Date_____

Sex (circle one) M F Other Information_____

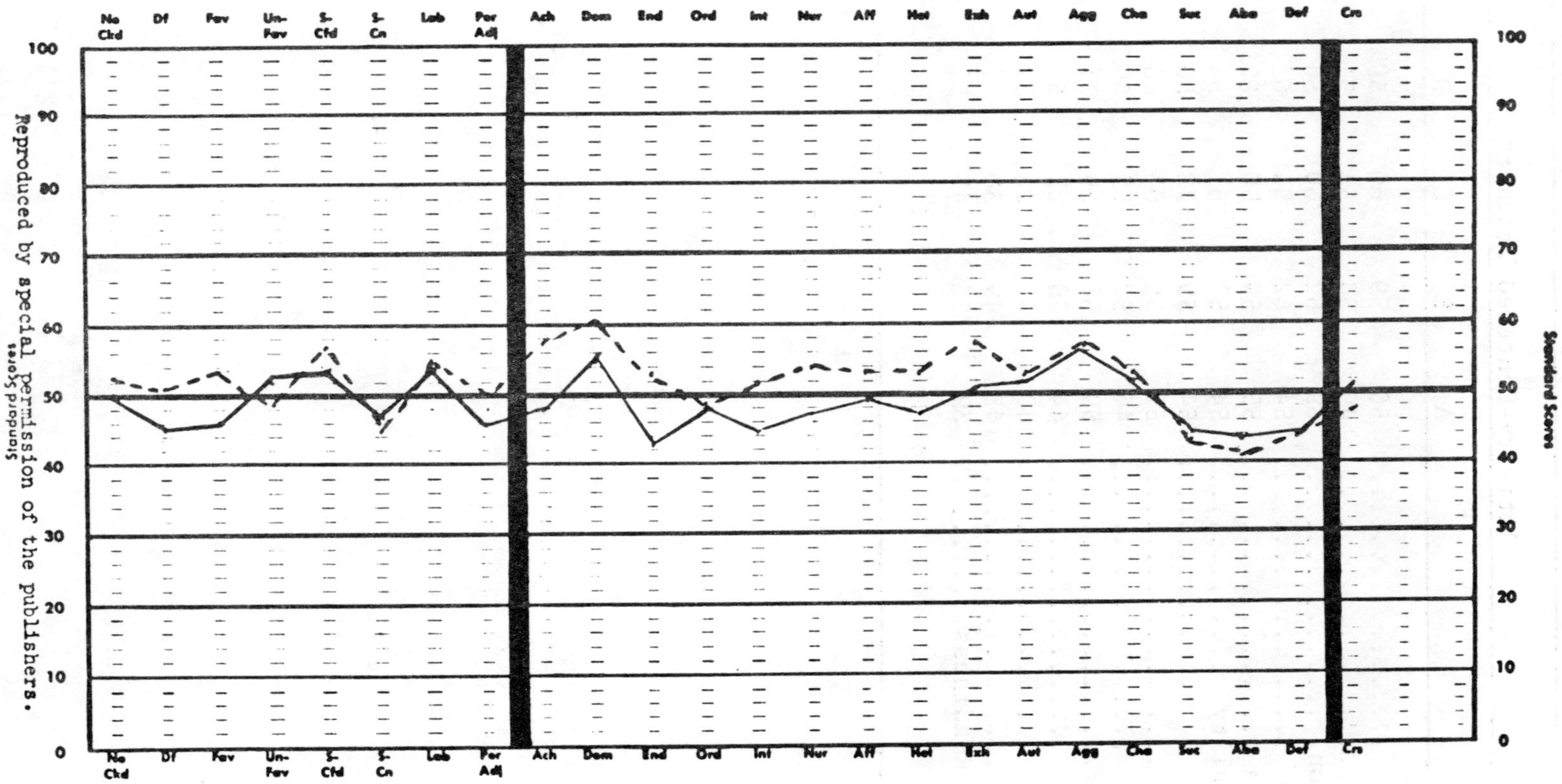

ACTIVITY-CENTERED -----
TRADITIONAL – – –

☐ Norm Table

Reproduced by special permission of the publishers.

Reproduced from the Manual for the Adjective Check List, by Harrison G. Gough, Ph.D. and Alfred B. Heilbrun Jr., Ph.D. Copyright 1965 by Consulting Psychologists Press, Inc.

determined to do well and usually succeeds. His motives are
internal and goal-centered rather than competitive, and in his
dealings with others he may actually be unduly trusting and
optimistic.[180]

The activity-centered teachers also scored higher than the traditional
teachers on the endurance scale with a mean standard score of 54 as compared to a
mean standard score of 42.5 for the traditional teachers. The range of scores was
46-60 for the activity-centered group and 32-60 for the traditional group indicating
less variability among the activity-centered teachers (Table 20).

According to the Manual:

The subject high on endurance is typically self-controlled and
responsible, but also idealistic and concerned about truth and
justice. By nature conventional, he may nonetheless (because
of his sense of rectitude) find himself championing unconven-
tional ideas and unpopular causes.[181]

It was concluded, based on the data from The Adjective Check List, that
the personality profiles of the activity-centered and traditional teachers were
very similar. The greatest differences appeared on the achievement and endurance
scales in favor of the activity-centered teachers.

Post Personality Profiles of Teachers

The same procedures were followed in developing profiles for the post
test. The individual teacher's standard scores and the group means on each of
the scales are reported in Table 21. On the basis of these data personality profiles for both groups of teachers were plotted. Figure 2 shows the profiles on
the post test. Again as occurred with the pre test, the profiles for both groups
of teachers were very similar. The greatest difference appeared on the scale
dealing with the total number of adjectives checked. On this scale the activity-
centered teachers obtained a mean standard score of 57.83 with a range of 51-68.
The traditional teachers had a mean of 46.33 with a range of 37-67, indicating
greater variability in the scores in that group.

According to The Adjective Check List Manual:

Checking many adjectives seems to reflect surgency and drive, and
a relative absence of repressive tendencies. Correlation with intelligence is slightly negative, so that the exuberance in behavior
may possibly spring more from shallowness and inattention to ambigui-
ties than from a deep level of involvement. The individual high on
this variable tends to be described as emotional, adventurous, whole-
some, conservative, enthusiastic, unintelligent, frank and helpful.
He is active, apparently means well, but tends to blunder.[182]

It was concluded that the personality profiles of the activity-centered
and traditional teachers were very similar at the end of the school year. The
greatest difference appeared on the number of adjectives checked in favor of the
activity-centered teachers.

Table 21 presents the post standard scores on each scale for every teacher
in the study and the arithmetic mean standard score for the activity-centered and
traditional teachers.

TABLE 21

PRE ADJECTIVE CHECK LIST STANDARD SCORES AND MEANS

Traditional Teachers

	A	B	C	D	E	F	Mn.
Number of Adjectives Checked	67	47	37	45	38	44	46.33
Defensiveness	61	51	41	57	36	55	50.16
Number of Favorable Adjectives Checked	63	51	41	56	39	64	52.33
Number of Unfavorable Adjectives Checked	40	42	73	42	59	43	49.83
Self-confidence	59	43	62	72	53	50	56.5
Self-control	58	56	31	47	41	55	48.
Lability	53	45	55	68	48	78	57.83
Personal Adjustment	61	53	28	51	46	57	49.33
Achievement	59	48	57	57	40	45	51.
Dominance	65	39	62	68	46	46	54.33
Endurance	60	55	43	64	41	41	50.66
Order	53	55	40	62	34	42	47.66
Intraception	56	60	21	72	34	55	49.66
Nurturance	58	57	30	52	37	65	49.83
Affiliation	65	49	34	55	37	56	49.33
Heterosexuality	58	54	52	56	46	61	54.66
Exhibition	60	40	65	56	49	49	53.16
Autonomy	61	41	72	59	49	54	56.
Aggression	47	40	75	55	60	49	54.33
Change	54	42	68	61	45	75	57.5
Succorance	36	50	46	33	42	83	48.33
Abasement	43	59	24	40	43	51	43.33
Deference	45	62	16	39	48	57	44.5
Counseling Readiness	51	29	69	59	49	52	51.5

Activity-Centered Teachers

	A	B	C	D	E	F	Mn.
Number of Adjectives Checked	63	52	68	55	51	58	57.83
Defensiveness	57	64	59	54	31	47	52.
Number of Favorable Adjectives Checked	55	72	62	54	44	41	54.66
Number of Unfavorable Adjectives Checked	38	38	42	44	61	53	49.33
Self-confidence	61	62	74	36	34	57	54.
Self-control	59	62	49	54	51	83	5-.33
Lability	39	54	59	59	56	50	52.83
Personal Adjustment	53	65	63	40	41	49	51.83
Achievement	67	67	63	53	42	62	59.
Dominance	62	65	68	61	39	61	59.33

Table 21 (Continued)

	Activity-Centered Teachers						
	A	B	C	D	E	F	Mn.
Endurance	65	61	62	48	34	54	54.
Order	57	57	59	52	43	50	53.
Intraception	49	63	58	53	42	48	52.16
Nurturance	63	58	51	49	43	59	53.83
Affiliation	65	66	50	42	41	59	53.83
Heterosexuality	58	54	61	48	34	54	51.5
Exhibition	51	56	68	42	51	59	54.5
Autonomy	47	50	57	47	45	47	48.83
Aggression	49	52	57	52	60	69	56.5
Change	46	48	62	35	53	63	51.16
Succorance	42	39	34	45	56	51	47.83
Abasement	44	42	30	50	67	33	44.33
Deference	55	53	24	61	44	40	46.16
Counseling Readiness	43	35	51	44	46	50	44.83

FIGURE 2
PROFILE SHEET FOR THE ADJECTIVE CHECK LIST
POST PERSONALITY PROFILE

Name_____ Age_____ Date_____

Sex (circle one) M F Other Information_____

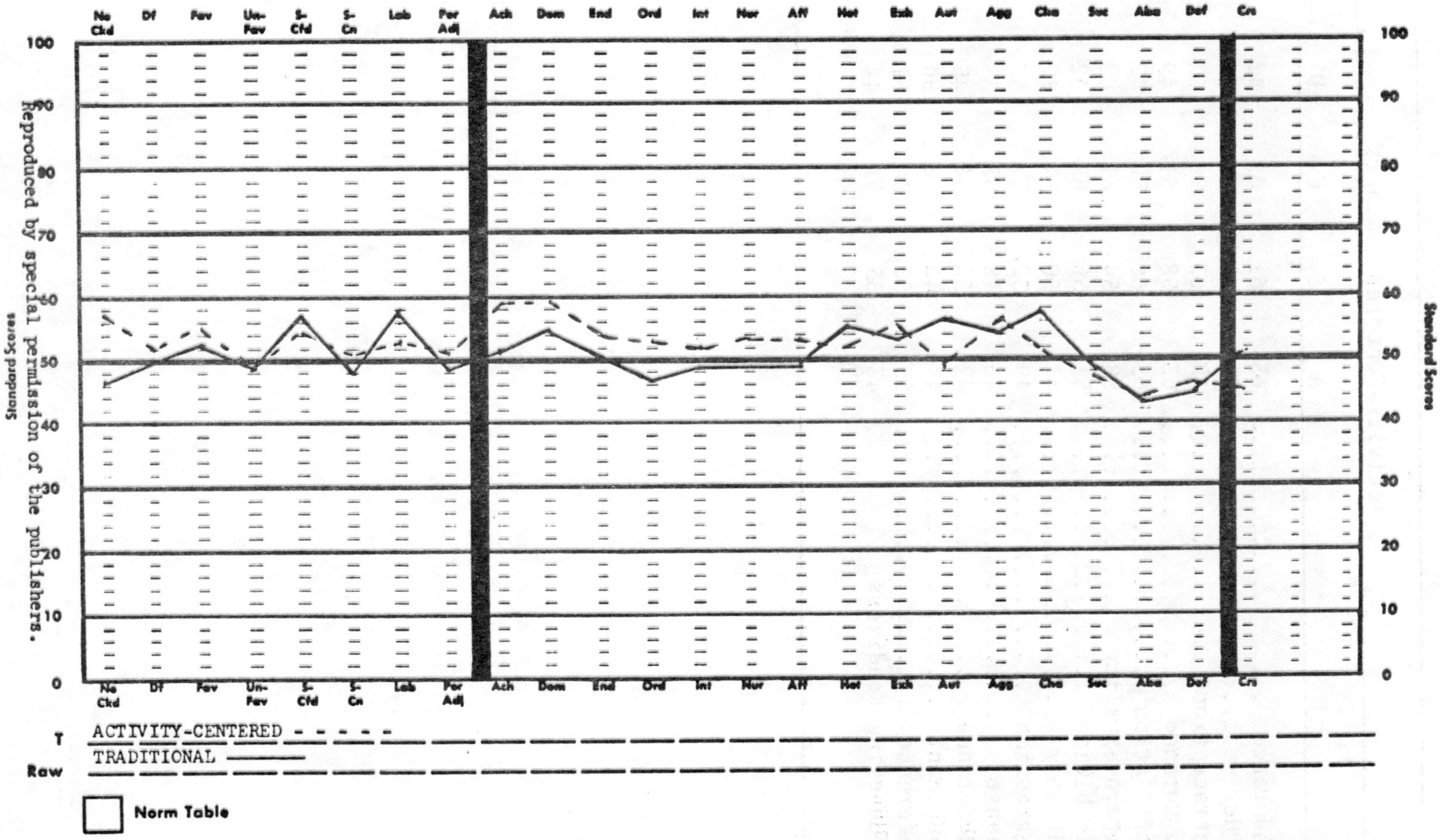

ACTIVITY-CENTERED – – – –
TRADITIONAL ————

☐ Norm Table

Reproduced from the Manual for the Adjective Check List, by Harrison O. Gough, Ph.D. and Alfred B. Heilbrun Jr., Ph.D. Copyright 1965 by Consulting Psychologists Press, Inc.

Reproduced by special permission of the publishers.

Changes in Personality Profiles

In comparing the pre and post test profiles, the greatest changes occurred on the scales dealing with the number of adjectives checked, endurance, autonomy and change.

Table 22 presents a summary of the pre and post mean standard scores for each of the twenty-four scales of The Adjective Check List for both the activity-centered and traditional teachers.

At the beginning of the school year, there was a difference of 2.85 between the means of the two groups of teachers on the total number of adjectives checked (activity-centered 52.83, traditional 50). At the end of the school year, the difference between the two means was 10.53 (activity-centered 57.83, traditional 46.33). This reflects a marked change in the two groups of teachers.

The difference between the two groups on endurance shifted from a spread of 10.5 (activity-centered 53, traditional 42.5) to a diminution in difference between the means of 3.44 (activity-centered 54, traditional 50.66) indicating that the two groups of teachers were much closer together on this scale at the end of the year.

On the scales of autonomy and change both groups of teachers had nearly equal mean standard scores at the beginning of the year (autonomy 53 and 52.66, change 53 and 52.5). At the end of the year the group of traditional teachers had higher mean scores on both scales which indicated moderate change (autonomy: traditional 56, activity-centered 48.83, and change: traditional 57.5, activity-centered 51.16).

The achievement scale mean scores changed somewhat. At the beginning of the year the difference between mean scores was 10 (activity-centered 58.83, traditional 48.83). At the end of the year the difference between mean scores was 8 (activity-centered 59, traditional 51).

It was concluded that the greatest changes which occurred were on the number of adjectives checked and on endurance. There were moderate changes on the autonomy and change scales.

Classroom Observations

To assure the fact that both groups of teachers were adhering to their organizational patterns, classroom observations were conducted both formally and informally. In the latter instance, observations were undertaken as the investigator administered the self-concept tests to individual children in the classroom setting. In addition, three formal observations of approximately on hour's duration were undertaken in each of the classrooms from November to March. On these occasions the investigator recorded her findings on the check list, "Your Classroom As You See It" (Appendix pp. 92-96).

Based on her observations, the investigator was satisfied that each teacher adhered to the organizational plan to which she was assigned. Major differences between the two types of classrooms were clearly exhibited in the areas of; physical environment, classroom management and classroom climate.

The traditional classrooms were more structured, teacher-directed, and

TABLE 22

PRE AND POST MEAN STANDARD SCORES ON THE ADJECTIVE CHECK LIST

	Pre Test	
	Activity-Centered Teachers	Traditional Teachers
Number of Adjectives Checked	52.83	50.
Defensiveness	51.83	45.83
Number of Favorable Adjectives Checked	53.66	46.
Number of Unfavorable Adjectives Checked	49.33	52.16
Self-confidence	57.33	53.5
Self-control	46.66	47.66
Lability	55.16	54.5
Personal Adjustment	50.5	46.83
Achievement	58.83	48.83
Dominance	60.16	54.5
Endurance	53.	42.5
Order	49.3	48.16
Intraception	52.	45.33
Nurturance	54.16	46.5
Affiliation	53.66	48.5
Heterosexuality	53.66	47.33
Exhibition	57.83	51.16
Autonomy	53.	52.66
Aggression	56.83	57.16
Change	53.	52.5
Succorance	43.83	45.83
Abasement	41.16	43.33
Deference	44.83	44.66
Counseling Readiness	47.	51.5

	Post Test	
	Activity-Centered Teachers	Traditional Teachers
Number of Adjectives Checked	57.83	46.33
Defensiveness	52.	50.16
Number of Favorable Adjectives Checked	54.66	52.33
Number of Unfavorable Adjectives Checked	49.33	49.83
Self-confidence	54.	56.5
Self-control	51.33	48.
Lability	52.83	57.83
Personal Adjustment	51.83	49.33
Achievement	59.	51.
Dominance	59.33	54.33

Table 22 (Continued)

	Post Test	
	Activity-Centered Teachers	Traditional Teachers
Endurance	54.	50.66
Order	53.	47.66
Intraception	52.16	49.66
Nurturance	53.83	49.83
Affiliation	53.83	49.33
Heterosexuality	51.5	54.66
Exhibition	54.5	53.16
Autonomy	48.83	56.
Aggression	56.5	54.33
Change	51.16	57.5
Succorance	47.83	48.83
Abasement	44.33	43.33
Deference	46.16	44.5
Counseling Readiness	44.83	51.5

adhered to regular schedules. Children in five of these classrooms sat in rows throughout the year, thus minimizing the possibility of peer interaction. Reading was conducted in small groups in a selected corner of the classroom.

There was an air of informality and freedom in the activity-centered classrooms. These rooms had a wide variety of interest and learning centers. Children were free to move about the room, work as individuals or in small groups of their peers. As the year progressed, the children were given more freedom in the planning of their own day. The teacher's role, in each instance, continued to be that of facilitator of learning. Reading was taught in a variety of ways, with a variety of materials depending on the needs and learning style of each child.

Materials Questionnaire

To control for the possibility that the activity-centered classrooms might be more adequately equipped with instructional materials in the area of reading, all teachers in both types of classrooms were asked to complete a questionnaire designed to secure this information (Appendix p.97).

A summary of the teachers' responses is reported in Table 23.

TABLE 23

INSTRUCTIONAL MATERIALS AVAILABLE

Material	Activity-Centered Classrooms	Traditional Classrooms
Basal Readers	6	6
Supplementary Basals	6	5
High-Interest Low Vocabulary Books	5	4
Library Books	6	6
Trade Books	6	5
General Skills Workbooks	6	6
Phonics Workbooks	6	6
Commercially Prepared Dittos	6	6
Filmstrips	6	6
Records	6	5
Commercially Prepared Reading Games	6	6
Manipulatives	6	3
Reading Kits	2	4

When the teachers' responses were analyzed on a classroom by classroom basis it was found that all of the inventoried materials were available in two of the activity-centered classrooms. Of the remaining four classrooms, three were lacking in reading kits, and one was lacking in high interest - low vocabulary books as well as reading kits.

All of the inventoried materials were available in three of the traditional classrooms. Of the remaining three classrooms, one was lacking: high interest - low vocabulary books; trade books; manipulatives; and reading kits. The remaining classroom was lacking in manipulatives only.

On the basis of this information, it was concluded that although reading kits were unavailable in more of the activity-centered classrooms, two of the traditional classrooms were generally less well-equipped with instructional materials.

All of the teachers were polled regarding their satisfaction with the ability of the materials available to them to meet the special needs of the children in the classrooms.

Table 24 reports a summary of their responses.

TABLE 24

TEACHER ATTITUDE TOWARD MATERIALS AVAILABLE

Material	Activity-Centered				
	Excellent	Good	Poor	Material not Available	No Comment
Basal Readers		1	5		
Supplementary Basals		1	5		
High Interest-Low Vocabulary	2	3		1	
Library Books	2	1	3		
Trade Books	2	1	3		
General Skills Workbooks		4	2		
Phonics Workbooks	1	3	2		
Commercially Prepared Dittos		3	3		
Filmstrips	2	2	2		
Records	3	2	1		
Commercially Prepared Reading Games	2	4			
Manipulatives	4	1	1		
Reading Kits				2	4

Material	Traditional				
	Excellent	Good	Poor	Material not Available	No Comment
Basal Readers	1	3	2		
Supplementary Basals	1	3	1	1	
High Interest-Low Vocabulary	1	2		2	1
Library Books	3	2			1
Trade Books		2	1	1	2
General Skills Workbooks	1	5			
Phonics Workbooks	1	5			
Commercially Prepared Dittos	1	4			1
Filmstrips	1	3			2
Records	2	2		1	1
Commercially Prepared Reading Games	4	2			
Manipulatives	1	2		3	
Reading Kits	1		2	2	1

An analysis of the teachers' responses to this item on the questionnaire indicated that both the activity-centered and traditional teachers were satisfied with the following types of materials in their ability to meet the special needs of the children in three classrooms: high interest - low vocabulary books; library books; general skills workbooks; phonics workbooks; commercially prepared dittos; reading games; records; and manipulatives. The major difference of opinion was in regard to the basal reader. In this instance the majority of the activity-centered teachers were dissatisfied, while the majority of the traditional teachers were dissatisfied.

All teachers in both groups felt that it was necessary to supplement the classroom materials in order to better meet the special needs of the children in their classrooms. In addition all teachers in both groups found it necessary to adjust their teaching methods in an attempt to better meet the needs of individual children. The traditional teachers stated that they spent more time with their slower readers, provided more practice and drill, and incorporated phonics into the regular program. The activity-centered teachers stated that they endeavored to meet special needs by providing materials which matched the learning styles of individual children; integrating the total language arts program through frequent use of language-experience stories, introducing new skills in small group situations, encouraging peer learning and utilizing parent volunteers.

CHAPTER SUMMARY

Data provided by testing 257 first grade children, 133 of whom were in activity-centered classrooms and 124 of whom were in traditional classrooms, were statistically treated to yield answers to the questions of this study which investigated the relationship of self-concept and classroom organization to reading achievement in grade one.

The questions and sub-questions of this study and the answers provided by the statistical analysis follow.

Question 1: What is the relationship between pre self-concept and reading readiness?

Answer: It was found that there was no significant relationship between pre self-concept and reading readiness.

Question 2: What is the relationship between pre self-concept and reading achievement?

Answer: It was found that there was no significant relationship between pre self-concept and reading achievement.

    Question 2a: What is the interaction effect of pre self-concept and classroom organization on reading achievement?

    Answer: It was found that there was no significant interaction effect of classroom organization and pre self-concept on reading achievement. However, the activity-centered classrooms showed the higher adjusted mean score in reading achievement.

Question 3: What is the relationship between reading achievement and post self-concept.

Answer: It was found that there was no significant relationship between reading achievement and post self-concept.

Question 4: Will there be a difference between the post self-concept scores of children in the activity-centered classrooms and the post self-concept scores of children in the traditional classrooms?

Answer: It was found that there was a statistically significant difference at the .05 level between the total post self-concept scores of children in the activity-centered classrooms and the children in the traditional classrooms. The difference favored the activity-centered classrooms.

Question 4a: Will there be a difference between the post self-concept scores of children with high reading achievement scores and the post self-concept scores of children with low reading achievement scores?

Answer: It was found that there was no significant difference in the post self-concept scores of children with high reading achievement scores and the post self-concept scores of children with low reading achievement scores.

Question 4b: What is the interaction effect of classroom organization and reading achievement on post self-concept?

Answer: It was found that there was a statistically significant interaction effect at the .05 level of classroom organization and reading achievement on post self-concept. The variable of classroom organization was found to have a significant main effect at the .05 level on post self-concept. These data favored the activity-centered classrooms.

Question 5: What is the interaction effect of classroom organization and reading readiness on reading achievement?

Answer: It was found that there was no significant interaction effect of classroom organization and reading readiness on reading achievement. The variable of reading readiness was found to have a statistically significant main effect at the .05 level on reading achievement.

Question 5a: Will there be a difference between the reading achievement scores of children in the activity-centered classrooms and the reading achievement scores of children in the traditional classrooms?

Answer: It was found that there was no significant difference between the observed total reading achievement scores of children in the activity-centered classrooms and the observed total reading achievement scores of children in the traditional classrooms.

Question 5b: Will there be a difference between the reading achievement scores of those children who have high post self-concept scores and the reading achievement scores of those children who have low post self-concept scores?

Answer: It was found that there was no significant difference between the reading achievement scores of those children who have high post self-concept scores and those children who have low post self-concept scores.

Question 5c: What is the interaction effect of classroom organization and post self-concept on reading achievement?

Answer: It was found that there was no significant interaction effect of classroom organization and post self-concept on reading achievement.

The conclusions and implications for further research and teaching, suggested by the findings summarized above, are presented in Chapter V.

Footnotes:

174. Thomas, The Thomas Self-Concept Values Test.

175. Significance at .05 is 3.88.

176. Murphy and Durrell, The Murphy-Durrell Reading Readiness Analysis.

177. Durost et al., Metropolitan Achievement Tests.

178. Henry E. Garrett and R. S. Woodworth, Statistics in Psychology and Education (New York: David McKay Inc., 1965), pp. 451-454.

179. Gough and Heilburn, The Adjective Check List.

180. Gough and Heilburn, The Adjective Check List Manual, p. 7.

181. Ibid.

182. Ibid., p. 7.

CHAPTER V

SUMMARY AND IMPLICATIONS FOR FURTHER RESEARCH AND FOR TEACHING

Summary

The primary purpose of this study was to investigate and describe the relationships between and among classroom organization, self-concept and reading achievement. The study was conducted with twelve first grade classrooms, nine of which were located in the state of New Hampshire and three of which were located in the state of Maine. Six of these classrooms were organized according to traditional patterns, while the remaining six classrooms were activity-centered.

The total sample of 257 children, 133 in the activity-centered classrooms and 124 in traditional classrooms, was administered the following measures:

1. A group reading readiness test at the beginning of the school year

2. An individual self-concept test (a measure of the way the child sees himself, as well as the way he believes his mother, teacher and peers see him) at the beginning of the school year to obtain a pre self-concept measure and at the end of the school year to obtain a post self-concept measure

3. A group intelligence test

4. The reading subtests of the Metropolitan Achievement Test at the end of the school year

The data provided by testing the 257 children in the sample were statistically treated using Pearson product-moment correlation, analysis of variance and analysis of covariance.

Conclusions

An analysis of the initial data showed that there were no significant differences between the children in the activity-centered classrooms and the children in the traditional classrooms on the variables of age, sex, intelligence and pre self-concept.

Further analysis of the data enabled the investigator to answer the questions and sub-questions of the study as follows:

1. What is the relationship between pre self-concept and reading readiness?

There was no statistically significant relationship between pre self-concept and reading readiness. This finding held true on all of the correlations which were conducted on all of the subtests of The Thomas Self-Concept Values Test and the subtests of The Murphy-Durrell Reading Readiness Analysis. The correlation between the total pre self-concept test and the total reading readiness that was -.15. The correlations between the subtests of the pre self-concept test and the subtests of the reading readiness test ranged from -.09 to .16 indicating slightly negative correlations.

2. What is the relationship between pre self-concept and reading achievement?

There was no statistically significant relationship between pre self-concept and reading achievement. This finding was consistent on all of the subtests of The Thomas Self-Concept Values Test and the reading subtests of the Metropolitan Achievement Test. The correlation between the total pre self-concept test and the total reading achievement test was -.12. The correlations between the subtests of the pre self-concept test and the subtests of the reading achievement test ranged from -.01 to -.12 indicating slightly negative correlations.

   2a What is the interaction effect of pre self-concept and classroom organization on reading achievement?

It was found that there was no significant interaction effect of classroom organization and pre self-concept on reading achievement. Of the independent variables, pre self-concept showed the strongest main effect on reading achievement, although it was not statistically significant. Through the analysis of covariance the data revealed that:

    (1) the activity-centered classrooms yielded a higher adjusted mean reading achievement score (57.80) than the traditional classrooms (55.81)

    (2) the high pre self-concept group attained a higher adjusted mean reading achievement score (58.49) than the low pre self-concept group (55.11)

    (3) the activity-centered high pre self-concept group yielded a higher adjusted mean reading achievement score (60.12) than the traditional high pre self-concept group (56.87)

    (4) the activity-centered low pre self-concept group yielded a higher adjusted mean reading achievement score (55.48) than the traditional low pre self-concept group (54.75).

3. What is the relationship between reading achievement and post self-concept?

There was no statistically significant relationship between reading achievement and post self-concept. This finding held true on all of the correlations which were conducted on all of the subtests of The Thomas Self-Concept Values Test and the reading subtests of the Metropolitan Achievement Test. The correlation between the total post self-concept test and the total reading achievement test was -.14. The correlations between the subtests of the post self-concept test and the reading subtests of the achievement test ranged from +.04 to -.08.

4. Will there be a difference between the post self-concept scores of children in the activity-centered classrooms and the post self-concept scores of children in the traditional classrooms?

There was a statistically significant difference at the .05 level between the total post self-concept scores of children in the activity-centered classrooms and the total post self-concept scores of children in the traditional classrooms. The data favored the children in the activity-centered classrooms.

The data also revealed a statistically significant difference at the .05 level between the children in the activity-centered classroom and the children in the traditional classrooms on the self-as-subject subtest and the mother referent subtest. These data also favored the children in the activity-centered classrooms. Although the difference between groups on the teacher referent and peer referent subtests was not significant, the difference in each instance approached significance in favor of the children in the activity-centered classrooms.

4a. Will there be a difference between the post self-concept scores of children with high reading achievement scores and the post self-concept scores of children with low reading achievement scores?

There was a statistically significant difference at the .05 level between the total post self-concept scores of children in the activity-centered classrooms and the total post self-concept scores of the children in the traditional classrooms. The difference favored the activity-centered classrooms. In using the analysis of covariance the data also revealed that:

(1) the high reading achievement group showed the higher adjusted post self-concept mean (30.28) over the low reading achievement group (29.83)

(2) the activity-centered high reading achievement group showed the higher adjusted post self-concept mean (32.94) over the traditional high reading achievement group (27.62)

(3) the traditional low reading achievement group showed the higher adjusted post self-concept mean (30.03) over the activity-centered low reading achievement group (29.63)

4b. What is the interaction effect of classroom organization and reading achievement on post self-concept?

There was a statistically significant interaction effect at the .05 level of classroom organization and reading achievement on post self-concept. It was also found that classroom organization has a statistically significant main effect on post self-concept at the .05 level. These data favored the activity-centered classrooms.

5. What is the interaction effect of classroom organization and reading readiness on reaching achievement?

There was no statistically significant interaction effect of classroom organization and reading readiness on reading achievement. Of the independent variables, the variable of reading readiness was found to have a statistically significant main effect at the .005 level on reading achievement. Classroom organization did not affect reading achievement at a statistically significant level.

5a. Will there be a difference between the reading achievement scores of children in the activity-centered classrooms and the reading achievement scores of children in the traditional classrooms?

There was no significant difference between the observed reading achievement scores of children in the activity-centered classrooms and the observed reading achievement scores of children in the traditional classrooms.

5b. Will there be a difference between the reading achievement scores of those children who have high post self-concepts and those children who have low post self-concepts?

There was no significant difference between the reading achievement scores of those children who have high post self-concept scores and those children who have low post self-concept scores. In using the analysis of covariance the data also revealed that:

(1) the activity-centered classrooms showed the higher adjusted mean reading achievement score (57.81) over the traditional classrooms (55.52)

(2) The high post self-concept group showed a lower adjusted mean reading achievement score (56.08) than the low post self-concept group (57.24)

(3) the activity-centered high post self-concept group showed the higher adjusted mean score (58.45) over the traditional high post self-concept group (53.72)

(4) the activity-centered low post self-concept group showed a slightly lower adjusted mean reading achievement score (57.17) than the traditional low post self-concept group (57.32)

5c. What is the interaction effect of classroom organization and post self-concept on reading achievement?

While there was no significant interaction effect of classroom organization and post self-concept on reading achievement, it was found that the interaction of classroom organization and post self-concept had a strong effect on reading achievement with a $P = .09$ favoring the activity-centered high post self-concept group which showed the highest adjusted mean reading achievement score.

Classroom organization was also found to have a strong effect with a $P = .13$ favoring the activity-centered classrooms which showed an adjusted mean reading achievement score of 57.81 as compared to the adjusted mean reading achievement score of 55.52 for the traditional classrooms.

Based on the findings reported, the primary conclusion made in this study is that the activity-centered approach in comparison to the traditional approach has a greater positive impact on self-concept resulting in higher self-concepts. It is also concluded that the activity-centered approach as compared to the traditional results in reading achievement equal to or slightly better than reading achievement obtained in the traditional classroom when reading readiness and self-concept are held in control. This study then seems to empirically substantiate the claims of the advocates of activity-centered, informal education--i.e., that children experiencing this approach to education not only achieve as well as children in the traditional classrooms, but they also significantly improve their self-concept.

The findings of this study emerge as more compelling when one considers that the study sample consisted of first grade children whose self-concepts would be expected to change at a slow incremental rate. It seems reasonable to speculate that if first grade students in activity-centered classrooms show a statistically higher post self-concept at the end of the first year of school than first grade children in the traditional classrooms then over a period of three or four years the cumulative effect of annual gains in self-concept may result in a wide gap between the self-concepts of children in the activity-centered classrooms and the self-concepts of children in the traditional classrooms.

The same conjecture could also be applied to reading achievement. While the differences on this variable were not statistically significant, they did approach significance and it could be hypothesized that over a period of three or four years such differences could become significant.

Limitations of the study

In reaching conclusions there must be a consideration of the techniques and definitions used, the assumptions made, and the recognized limitations of the study. The limitations of this study involve limitations of place and sampling. This study can only indicate that certain statistical relationships exist among a sample of 257 first grade children drawn from twelve classrooms located in six communities in New Hampshire and two communities in Maine.

In order to measure self-concept, reading achievement and teacher personality and in order to assess the nature of classroom organization, it was necessary to use certain instruments and techniques designed to sample and reveal these phenomena. The investigator limits the findings of her study to the degree of validity these instruments and techniques possess.

Another limitation of the study is that the investigator could not control the data for the socio-economic influence of each community. Controls were not possible because the investigator had to work with classrooms which were available and accessible for research and which met the definitions of activity-centered and traditional classrooms.

It is generally accepted that self-concept changes slowly. A study of one year's duration may have limitations which could be compensated for through longitudinal studies of three to four years duration.

The study was limited to first grade children who because of their limited school differences may not have encountered the quantity of successful or unsuccessful experience in reading necessary to affect the self-concept.

Implications for further research

In the course of this study and its conclusion many suggestions come to mind which should be accomplished in order to add to knowledge of the relationships between classroom organization, reading achievement and self-concept. The recommendations for further study evolve from the limitations of this study. The following suggestions for further study are offered.

1. A similar study could be conducted using different measures of reading achievement, self-concept and classroom organization

2. A similar study could be conducted using different grade level samples (i.e., grade two, three, four, five, etc.)

3. A three or four year longitudinal type of study of self-concept, reading achievement and classroom organization could be conducted using case histories,

follow-up studies and observational techniques.

4. A similar study could be conducted on the relationships between classroom organization, self-concept, and other measures of academic achievement (i.e., mathematics, social studies, science, etc.)

5. A study could be conducted of the relationships between teacher personality, self-concept and reading achievement

6. A study could be conducted of the relationships between parental social class status, self-concept and reading achievement

7. A similar study could be conducted in a large urban community

8. An intensive anthropological study could be conducted on one school and its effect on self-concept and reading achievement

9. A similar study could be conducted with a preschool sample of children

10. A study could be conducted of the relationships between sociometic status of the child and self-concept and reading achievement

11. A study could be conducted of the relationships between teacher-pupil interactions and self-concept and reading achievement

12. A study could be conducted of the impact of counseling and its effect on reading achievement

Implications for teaching

Since this investigation supports the hypothesis that within the scope of this study activity-centered, informal education enhances the self-concept and produces reading achievement scores equal to or slightly higher than those obtained by children in traditional classrooms, first grade teachers may consider this approach to classroom organization a viable alternative.

It must be recognized, however, that the activity-centered classrooms which were utilized in this investigation were carefully planned, well-organized, and functioning at a high degree of excellence. Their effectiveness was likely due to the fact that the teachers in these classrooms were not only well-trained in and committed to the philosophy of informal education, but also knowledgeable of a wide variety of approaches which can be implemented in translating the theory of informal education into practice. In addition, the investigator considers it extremely important to note that these teachers voluntarily chose to implement this approach and availed themselves of a university program which assisted them in that endeavor.

To aid teachers who wish to utilize this alternative, teacher educators might consider:

1. providing field-based programs which offer teachers opportunities to gain expertise and skill in this area. These programs should model activity-centered education themselves.

2. forming an Informal Education Advisory Service which consists of faculty members who would be available to public school teachers who do not wish

to enter degree programs but are desirous of implementing informal education. In this instance assistance would be provided on site and supplemented on campus when appropriate.

3. helping teachers to develop and expand as persons and actualize their own potential.

4. developing in teachers a sensitivity to and an awareness of the child's self-concept. Facilitative approaches and materials which enhance the child's image of himself and his sensitivity to others should be integral parts of teacher education programs.

APPENDIX

OBSERVATIONAL INSTRUMENT USED IN
SELECTING THE TRADITIONAL TEACHERS

I. Identification

    Teachers' Name: _____
    School: _____
    Subject(s) Observed: _____
    Length of Observation: _____

II. Rating Scale

    1. Unsatisfactory   2. Marginal   3. Competent
    4. Above Average   3. Outstanding   6. Not Observed

III. RATING FACTORS

    A. <u>Classroom Atmosphere</u> | 1 | 2 | 3 | 4 | 5 | 6 |

        1. Observer's first impression
        2. Classroom organization (physical)
        3. Transition (Teacher Organization)
        4. Motivation of Students
        5. Discipline (overall control)
        6. Evidence of planned learning
        7. Evidence of concomitant learning
           (desirable attitudes)

    B. <u>Classroom Performance</u>

        1. Evidence of planned instruction
        2. Variety of approach
        3. Student participation
        4. Provision for individual differences
        5. Delivery or presentation
        6. Knowledge of subject matter
        7. Innovations
        8. Utilization of resources

IV. OVERALL EVALUATION (Please rate this teacher in comparison with all others in similar situations within your experience.)

    1. Unsatisfactory   ( )   4. Above Average   ( )
    2. Marginal   ( )   5. Outstanding   ( )
    3. Effective and
       Competent   ( )

V. COMMENTS BY OBSERVER

Observer's Name _____ Date _____

Bank Street Follow Through, 1970　　　　　　　　　　　　　　Third Version

YOUR CLASSROOM AS YOU SEE IT

A SELF-STUDY FOR TEACHERS AND PARAPROFESSIONALS
(AIDES, ASSISTANTS OR ASSOCIATES)

Date checked _____　　Your title: Teacher _____
(to be filled out separately by　　　　　　　　　　Associate _____
each member of the team and then　　　　　　　　　Assistant _____
compared.)　　　　　　　　　　　　　　　　　　　　Aide _____

Please check each question at the right on a scale from 1 to 5 to indicate how far you think that you, your students and your classroom have moved in the direction indicated by the question. The least positive response is (1), the most positive is (5).

PHASE ONE: SETTING UP THE LEARNING SITUATION

	1	2	3	4	5

I. THE PHYSICAL ENVIRONMENT

A. Room Arrangement

1. Does your room make small group and individual activities possible? _____

2. Are interest centers arranged so as to suggest specific activities with the materials needed? _____

3. Are these changed as new interests arise? _____

4. Is there private space for the children's own things and adequate storage for general equipment? _____

5. Is there a partitioned area with minimum of interruption for a child who needs privacy? _____

B. Materials and Equipment

1. Is the supply adequate? _____

2. Are materials appropriate to the age group in size and complexity? _____

3. Are they selected and arranged so as to stimulate curiosity and experimentation? _____

4. Are there some "home-brew" materials, i.e. some teacher-made or child-made materials rather than commercial products only? _____

5. Are manipulative materials placed within easy reach of children so that they can select and replace them easily? _____

			1	2	3	4	5
B.		Materials and Equipment (Continued)					
	6.	Do the materials reflect the child's own world by having some familiar, recognizable objects among them?					
	7.	Do they also extend the child's world by having some new and exciting objects, particularly living plants and/or animals?					
C.		Displays					
	1.	Are displays at eye level of children when physical conditions of room permit?					
	2.	Is children's work displayed prominently and with respect for its importance?					
	3.	Are displays changed frequently i.e. at least every month or as new interests arise?					
	4.	Are displays real learning experiences?					
D.		Classroom Library					
	1.	Is there an adequate supply of books accessible to children in the classroom?					
	2.	Are the books appropriate to the age and current interests of the children?					
	3.	Are they changed as new interests develop?					
	4.	Are children encouraged to select books by themselves?					
	5.	Are adult books with highly provocative and/or beautiful illustrations included even if not appropriate in toto to the age group?					

II. CLASSROOM MANAGEMENT

A. Organization of Daily Schedule

1. Is the sequence of what happens through the day clear and understandable to the children?

2. Is it fairly easy to change the schedule if some unexpected and important learning experience becomes possible?

	1	2	3	4	5

B. Movement from One Activity to Another

1. Is movement of a group or the whole class to the next activity planned so that these transitions are smooth?

2. Is the equipment available for the next activity without wasted time and confusion?

3. Is very little direction by you necessary?

4. Are the directions which are, in fact, necessary clear and specific?

C. Grouping Arrangement

1. Are small group activities planned by classroom team at appropriate times and with realization of how long children can concentrate?

2. Are there frequent one-to-one contacts between you and children?

3. Are one-to-one contacts among children encouraged?

4. Are activities carried out by children, without your supervision, encouraged?

5. Are all these activities and contacts planned so that they have meaning and purpose instead of being aimless "hit-or-miss"?

6. Does amount of structured instruction for total group fit the children's attention span?

7. Does the total group also have periods for recreation and social activities?

D. Teamwork Among Adults

1. Do you and your teammates in the classroom show respect for one another?

2. Do you cooperate and plan together?

3. Do paraprofessionals work directly with children in learning-teaching situations?

4. Are they encouraged to make suggestions?

	D. Teamwork Among Adults (continued)	1	2	3	4	5
	5. Are the reasons given clearly when such suggestions are not appropriate?					
	6. Are the special skills and understandings of the pschologist, nurse, social worker and parent coordinator sought and applied to the work with individual children?					
	7. Do you see yourself as a learner who can learn not only from other adults but from children?					
1	8. Does the teaching team visit parents in their homes to listen and learn more about the children before trying to enlist the cooperation of the parents in the children's learning?					
	9. Are parents involved in school activities? in planning?					
	10. Is there two-way communication with community as well as with the parents, i.e. openness to the community representatives' ideas and reactions, as well as interpreting of the Follow Through program to them?					
	11. Are children part of the team, i.e., do they participate in planning and doing for the group?					

III. CLIMATE IN THE CLASSROOM

    A. Social Climate

        1. Is there a general feeling of being comfortable, easy, relaxed and natural?

        2. Is there a sense of helping each other, of waiting for one's turn -- even when one child is deeply absorbed in an activity -- of group living?

        3. Is there a sense of joy in the work to be done, of industriousness, or really taking an active part in their own learning by most of the children?

        4. Are children made aware of their own growth by your recognition of specific accomplishments?

        5. Are they developing inner sense of mastery, not entirely dependent on adult approval?

	1	2	3	4	5

B. **Methods of Control**

1. Do children take part in defining the problems which require control and in discussing the limits that seem to be necessary?

2. Do they understand that the limits are set <u>for</u> them and not <u>against</u> them?

3. Is there freedom of movement and freedom of choice within the agreed upon limits?

4. Is a reasonable amount of childlike behavior accepted, such as that amount of noise, messiness, etc., which does not prevent other children from doing their work?

5. When you must stop what is happening, do you do so calmly, firmly and equally for all children at all times?

6. Do you make the child feel he is still accepted as a person, even though his behavior at that moment is unacceptable?

7. Are children shifted out of situations where controls seem to be breakding down by suggesting other ways of working it out?

8. Is every example of inner control by a child recognized and thus encouraged?

9. Do you develop inner controls indirectly by feeding in new materials, new ideas, new ways of working that will capture the imagination of the children and minimize the need for "acting out"?

10. Do you organize the small stops of learning, so that the child will be able to see how he is doing and will be motivated to further effort?

Questionnaire

Name

Date

1. Please indicate which of the following reading materials are available in your classroom for purposes of conducting your reading program.

   _____ basal readers
   _____ supplementary basals
   _____ high interest-low vocabulary books
   _____ library books
   _____ trade books
   _____ general skills workbooks
   _____ phonics workbooks
   _____ dittos
   _____ filmstrips
   _____ records
   _____ reading games
   _____ manipulatives
   _____ reading kits (e.g. SRA)

2. Please indicate how you rate each of the materials available to you in their ability to meet the special needs of the children in your classroom.

Material	Exc.	Good	Poor	Material	Exc.	Good	Poor
Basal readers				phonics workbooks			
supplementary basals				dittos			
high interest-low vocabulary books				records			
				filmstrips			
library books				reading games			
trade books				manipulatives			
general skills workbooks				reading kits			

3. Have you found it necessary to supplement the school provided materials in order to better meet the special needs of the children in your classroom?

   _____ Yes   _____ No   _____ Sometimes

4. Have you found it necessary to adjust your teaching methods in order to better meet the needs of individual children?

   _____ Yes   _____ No   _____ Sometimes

5. Please give some examples of the approaches you have employed in attempting to better meet the special needs of the children in your classroom.

BIBLIOGRAPHY

Abrams, Jules C. "A Study of Certain Personality Characteristics of Non-Readers and Achieving Readers." <u>Dissertation Abstracts</u>, 16, Ann Arbor, Michigan: University Microfilms, a Xerox Company, 1956.

Acinapuro, Philip J. "A Comparative Study of the Results of Two Reading Programs-- An Individualized Pattern and a Three Group Pattern." Ed.D dissertation, Teachers College, Columbia University, 1959.

Adams, Phyllis. "An Investigation of an Individualized Reading Program and a Modified Basal Reading Program in First Grade." Ed.D. dissertation, University of Denver, 1962.

Ames, Louise B., and Walker, Richard N. "Prediction of Later Reading Ability from Kindergarten Rorschach and IQ Scores." <u>The Journal of Educational Research</u> 55 (December 1964):309-313.

Anderson, Irving H. et al. "The Relationship between Reading Achievement and the Method of Teaching Reading." <u>University of Michigan School of Education Bulletin</u> 38 (May 1961):320-327.

Aspy, David N., and Roebuck, Flora N. "An Investigation of the Relationship Between Student Levels of Cognitive Functioning and the Teacher's Classroom Behavior." <u>The Journal of Educational Research</u> 65 (April 1972):365-368.

Athey, Irene J. "Reading-Personality Patterns at the Junior High School Level." <u>Dissertation Abstracts,</u> 26, Ann Arbor, Michigan: University Microfilms, a Xerox Company, 1966.

Bank Street Follow Through. "Your Classroom As You See It." New York, 1970. (Mimeographed.)

Baraffi, Gino. "The Effect of Two Types of Summer School Intervention on Self-Concept and Academic Achievement of Children of Seasonal and Migrant Workers." <u>Dissertation Abstracts</u>, 31, Ann Arbor, Michigan: University Microfilms, a Xerox Company, 1970-1971.

Bazemore, Judith S. <u>The Relationship between Student Level of Tension, the Learning Environment and Achievement in Reading</u>. Bethesda, Md.: ERIC Document Reproduction Service, ED 070 038, 1971.

Bell, Bruce B.; Anderson, Robert F.; and Lewis, Franklin D. "Some Personality and Motivational Factors in Reading Retardation." <u>The Journal of Educational Research</u> 65 (January 1972):229-233.

Beller, E. Kuno. "Research on Organized Programs of Early Education." <u>In Second Handbook of Research on Teaching</u>, pp. 530-600. Edited by Robert M. W. Travers. Chicago: Rand McNally and Company, 1973.

Blackman, George J. "A Clinical Study of the Personality Structure and Adjustment of Pupils Underachieving and Overachieving in Reading." Ed.D. dissertation, Cornell University, 1965.

Blanchard, Phyllis. "Psychoanalytic Contributions to the Problems of Reading Disabilities." The Psychoanalytic Study of the Child 2 (April 1946):163-187.

_____. "Reading Disabilities in Relation to Difficulties of Personality and Emotional Development." Mental Hygiene 20 (July 1936): 384-413.

_____. "Reading Disabilities in Relation to Maladjustment." Mental Hygiene 12 (July 1928):772-788.

Bodwin, Raymond. "The Relationship between Immature Self-Concept and Certain Emotional Disabilities." Dissertation Abstracts, 19, Ann Arbor, Michigan: University Microfilms, a Xerox Company, 1939.

Boleo, Angelo S. "Relationship of Change in Children's Self-Concept to Teacher Participation in a Child Study Program." Dissertation Abstracts, 28, Ann Arbor, Michigan: University Microfilms, a Xerox Company, 1967-1968.

Bond, Guy L. First Grade Reading Studies: An Overview. Elementary English 63 (May 1966):464-470.

Bonhorst, Ben A., and Sellers, Sophia. "Individualized Reading Vs. Textbook Instruction." Elementary English 36 (March 1959):185-190.

Boy, Angelo V., and Pine, Gerald J. Expanding the Self: Personal Growth for Teachers. Dubuque, Iowa: Wm. C. Brown Company, 1971.

Braidford, Margaret. "A Comparison of Two Teaching Methods, Individual and Group, in the Teaching of Comprehension in Beginning Reading." Ed.D. dissertation, New York University, 1960.

Bricklin, Patricia. "Self-Related Concepts and Aspiration Behavior of Achieving Readers and Two Types of Non-Achieving Readers." Dissertation Abstracts, 26, Ann Arbor, Michigan: University Microfilms, a Xerox Company, 1965.

Brown, Jeanette. "The Impact of Teacher Consultation on the Self-Perceptions of Elementary Children." Education 93 (April-May 1972):339-345.

Carlton, Leslie. "A Report of Self-Directive Dramatization in the Regular Elementary Classroom and Relationships Discovered with Progress in Reading Achievement and Self-Concept Changes." Dissertation Abstracts, 24, Ann Arbor, Michigan: University Microfilms, a Xerox Company, 1963-1964.

Carter, Cleo D. "The Relationship between Personality and Academic Achievement of Seven Year Olds." Ed.D. dissertation, Indiana University, 1953.

Chall, Jeanne, and Feldman, Shirley. "First Grade Reading: An Analysis of the Interaction of Professed Methods, Teacher Implementation and Child Backgrounds." The Reading Teacher 19 (May 1966):569-575.

Chronister, Glen M. "Personality and Reading Achievement." Elementary School Journal 64 (February 1964):253-260.

Coller, Allan R. The Assessment of Self-Concept in Early Childhood Education, Urbana, Illinois: ERIC Clearing House in Early Childhood Education, 1971.

Combs, Arthur. "A Perceptual View of the Adequate Personality." *Perceiving Behaving Becoming*, in *1962 Yearbook of the Association for Supervision and Curriculum Development*. Washington, D.C.: National Education Association, 1962.

_____. "New Horizons in Field Research." *Educational Leadership* 15 (February 1958):315-316.

_____, and Snygg, Donald. *Individual Behavior: A Perceptual Point of View*. New York: Harper and Brothers, 1959.

Cummings, Ruby N. "A Study of the Relationship between Self-Concept and Reading Achievement at Third Grade Level." *Dissertation Abstracts*, 31, Ann Arbor, Michigan: University Microfilms, a Xerox Company, 1970-1971.

Cynog, Frances. "Self-Selection in Reading: Report of a Longitudinal Study." In *Reading and the Elementary School Child*. Edited by Virgil M. Howes and Helen Fisher Darrow. New York: The Macmillan Company, 1958.

Davidson, Helen, and Lang, Gerhard. "Children's Perception of Their Teachers' Feelings toward Them Related to Self-Perception, School Achievement and Behavior." *Journal of Experimental Education* 29 (December 1960):107-118.

Douglas, Malcolm P., ed. *Claremont Reading Conference, Thirty-Second Yearbook*. California: Claremont Graduate School Curriculum Laboratory, 1968.

Doyle, Wayne J. *Teacher Perceptions: Do They Make a Difference?* Bethesda, Md.: ERIC Document Reproduction Service, ED 048 109, 1971.

Duker, Sam. "Needed Research in Individualized Reading." *Elementary English* 43 (March 1966):220-225.

Durost, Walter N. et al. *Metropolitan Achievement Tests*. Rev. Ed., Primary 1, Form F. New York: Harcourt Brace Javonovich, Inc., 1970.

_____. *Metropolitan Achievement Tests, Primary I Teacher's Handbook*. New York: Harcourt Brace Javonovich, Inc., 1971.

Durr, William S., and Schmatz, Robert R. "Personality Differences Between High-Achieving and Low-Achieving Gifted Children" *The Reading Teacher* 17 (January 1964):251-254.

Ebel, Robert L., ed. *Encyclopedia of Educational Research*. 4th ed. Toronto: The Macmillan Company, 1969.

Evans, Judith. *Interpersonal Self-Fulfilling Prophecies: Further Explorations from the Laboratory to the Classroom*. Bethesda, Md.: ERIC Document Reproduction Service, ED 014 900, 1969.

Flemming, Elyse S. *Teacher Expectancy or My Fair Lady*. Bethesda, Md.: ERIC Document Reproduction Service, ED 038 183, 1970.

Fox, Gudelia A., and Fox, Raymond B. "The Individualized Reading Controversy", *National Elementary School Principal* 44 (March 1965):258-260.

Frost, Barry P. "Some Personality Characteristics of Poor Readers." *Psychology in the Schools* 1-2 (July 1965):218-219.

Gage, Nathaniel L., ed. *Handbook of Research on Teaching*. Chicago: Rand McNally and Company, 1963.

Garrett, Henry E., and Woodworth, R.S. *Statistics in Psychology and Education*. New York: David McKay Company, Inc., 1958.

Gates, Arthur I. "The Role of Personality Maladjustment in Reading Disability." *Journal of Genetic Psychology* 59 (June 1941):77-83.

Giuliani, George A. "The Relationship of Self-Concept and Verbal-Mental Ability to Levels of Reading Rediness Amongst Kindergarten Children." *Dissertation Abstracts*, 28, Ann Arbor, Michigan: University Microfilms, a Xerox Company, 1968.

Glick, Oren. "Some Social-Emotional Consequences of Early Inadequate Acquisition of Reading Skills." *Journal of Educational Psychology* 63 (June 1972):253-257.

Goddard, Nora L. *Reading in the Modern Infant School*. London: University of London Press Ltd., 1969.

Goldsmith, Josephine. *The Effect of a High Expectancy on Reading Achievement and IQ of Students in Grade Ten*. Bethesda, Md.: ERIC Reproduction Service, ED 049 901, 1971.

Good, Thomas I. *Do Boys and Girls Receive Equal Opportunity in First Grade Reading Instruction?* Bethesda, Md.: ERIC Document Reproduction Service, ED 041 848, 1969.

Gough, Harrison G., and Heilburn, Alfred B. *The Adjective Check List*. Palo Alto, California: Consulting Psychologist Press, 1952.

_____. *The Adjective Check List Manual*. Palo Alto, California; Consulting Psychologists Press, 1965.

Hake, James M. "Covert Motivation of Good and Poor Readers." *The Reading Teacher* 22 (May 1969):731-738, 741.

Hallock, George A. "Attitudinal Factors Affecting Achievement in Reading." *Dissertation Abstracts*, 18, Ann Arbor, Michigan: University Microfilms, a Xerox Company, 1958.

Hamachek, Don E. *Encounters with the Self*. New York: Holt Rinehart and Winston, Inc., 1971.

Harckman, Laura D. *The Effect of Informal and Formal British Infant Schools on Reading Achievement*. Bethesda, Md.: ERIC Document Reproduction Service,

Harris, Albert J. "The Effective Teacher of Reading." *The Reading Teacher* 23 (December 1969):195-204.

_____, and Morrison, Coleman. "The CRAFT Project: A Final Report." *The Reading Teacher* 22 (January 1969):335-340.

Harris, Chester D. "The Psychology of Reading." *The Journal of Educational Research* 67 (May-June 1974):403-411.

Heathers, Glenn. "Grouping." In *Encyclopedia of Educational Research*, pp. 564-568. Edited by Robert L. Ebel. Toronto: The Macmillan Company, 1969.

Heilman, Arthur W. *Principles and Practices of Teaching Reading*. 3rd ed. Columbus, Ohio: Charles E. Merrill Publishing Co., 1972.

Holzinger, Margalith. "Personality and Behavioral Characteristics of Able and Less Able Readers of Elementary School Age." *Dissertation Abstracts*, 28, Ann Arbor, Michigan: University Microfilms, a Xerox Company, 1967-1968.

Howes, Virgil M., and Darrow, Helen Fisher, eds. *Reading and the Elementary School Child*. New York: The Macmillan Company, 1968.

Izzo, Ruth K. "A Comparison of Two Teaching Methods, Individual and Group, in The Teaching of Word Identification in Beginning Reading." Ed.D. dissertation, New York University, 1960.

Johnson, Rodney. "Individualized and Basal Reading Programs." *Elementary English* 42 (December 1965):902-904, 915.

Jones, Sara. "A Comparison of Teacher and Student Perceptions of Interpersonal Relationships and Self-Concepts." *Dissertation Abstracts*, 34, Ann Arbor, Michigan: University Microfilms, a Xerox Company, 1974.

Kagan, Jerome. "Reflection-Impulsivity and Reading Ability in Primary Grade Children." *Child Development* 36 (1965):609-628.

Karr, Harold. "An Experiment with an Individualized Method of Teaching Reading." *The Reading Teacher* 18 (February 1967):174-177.

Kelley, Earl C. *Education for What is Real*. New York: Harper and Brothers, 1951.

Kunz, Jean A. "The Self-Concept of the Young Child As He Learns to Read." *Claremont Reading Conference, Thirty-Second Yearbook*. Edited by Malcolm P. Douglas. Claremont, California: Claremont Graduate School Curriculum Laboratory, 1968.

Lamy, Mary. "Relationship of Self-Perceptions of Early Primary Children to Achievement in Reading." *Dissertation Abstracts*, 24, Ann Arbor, Michigan: University Microfilms, a Xerox Company, 1963.

Lewis, Ruth W. "The Relationship of Self-Concept to Reading Achievement." *Dissertation Abstracts*, 34, Ann Arbor, Michigan: University Microfilms, a Xerox Company, 1974.

LoPresti, Peter J. "Teacher's Appraisal of the Personal and Social Adjustment of Fourth, Fifth and Sixth Graders as Compared with Self-Evaluations by the Pupils." *Dissertation Abstracts*, 26, Ann Arbor, Michigan: University Microfilms, a Xerox Company, 1966.

Lovinger, Sophie. *The Interplay of Some Ago Functions in Six Year Old Children*. Bethesda, Md.: ERIC Document Reproduction Service, ED 020, 005, 1967.

Lumpkin, Donovan. "The Relationship of Self-Concept to Achievement in Reading." *Dissertation Abstracts*, 19, Ann Arbor, Michigan: University Microfilms, a Xerox Company, 1959.

McChristey, Antoinette. "A Comparative Study Whether Self-Selection Reading Can Be Successfully Used at Second Grade Level." Ed.M. thesis, University of Southern California, 1957.

McDaniel, Sylvia P. "The Effects of Selected Teacher Personality Variables on Reading Readiness, Self-Concept, and Changes in IQ in Culturally Deprived Five-Year-Olds." *Dissertation Abstracts*, 31, Ann Arbor, Michigan: University Microfilms, a Xerox Company, 1970-1971.

Marani, Salvatore D. "The Effect of Methods of Teaching Reading on the Reading Achievement and Attitude toward Self or Delinquent Boys." *Dissertation Abstracts*, 32, Ann Arbor, Michigan: University Microfilms, a Xerox Company, 1971.

Marble, James M. "An Analysis of the Effectiveness of Individualized Reading Instruction upon the Self-Concepts of Disadvantaged Students with Reading Disabilities." *Dissertation Abstracts*, 34, Ann Arbor, Michigan: University Microfilms, a Xerox Company, 1974.

Maslow, Abraham. *Motivation and Personality*. New York: Harper and Brothers, 1959.

Monroe, Marion. *Children Who Cannot Learn to Read*. Chicago: University of Chicago Press, 1928.

_____. "Diagnosis and Treatment of Reading Disabilities." Educational *Diagnosis*, in *Thirty-fourth Yearbook of the National Society for the Study of Education,* pt. 1. Bloomington, Ill.: Public Service Publishing Co., 1935.

_____, and Backus B. *Remedial Reading: A Monograph in Character Education*. Boston: Houghton Mifflin Company, 1937.

Moustakas, Clark. *The Authentic Teacher*. Cambridge, Massachusetts: Howard A. Doyle Publishing Company, 1966.

Murphy, Helen A., and Durrell, Donald D. *Murphy-Durrell Reading Readiness Analysis*. New York: Harcourt, Brace & World, Inc., 1965.

_____. *Murphy-Durrell Reading Readiness Analysis Manual of Directions*. New York: Harcourt, Brace and World, Inc., 1965.

Nicholson, Liston O. "The Relationship Between Self-Concept and Reading Achievement." *Dissertation Abstracts,* 25, Ann Arbor, Michigan: University Microfilms, a Xerox Company, 1965.

Norman, Ralph D., and Daley, Marion F. "The Comparative Personality Adjustment of Superior and Inferior Readers." *Journal of Educational Psychology* 50 (February 1959):31-36.

Paddleford, William B. "The Influence of Socio-economic Level, Sex and Ethnic Background Upon the Relationship Between Reading Achievement and Self-Concept." *Dissertation Abstracts*, 30, Ann Arbor, Michigan: University Microfilms, a Xerox Company, 1969-1970.

Palardy, J. Michael. "What Teachers Believe--What Children Achieve." *Elementary School Journal* 69 (April 1969):370-374.

Perkins, Hugh V. "Factors Influencing Change in Children's Self-Concepts." *Child Development* 29 (June 1958):221-230.

_____. "Teachers' and Peers' Perceptions of Children's Self-Concepts." *Child Development* 29 (June 1958):203-220.

Pintner, Rudolph; Cunningham, Bess V.; and Durost, Walter N. *Pintner-Cunningham Primary Test*. Rev. Ed., Form A. New York: Harcourt, Brace & World, Inc., 1964.

_____. *Pintner-Cunningham Primary Test Directions for Administering, Scoring and Interpreting*. New York: Harcourt, Brace & World, Inc., 1966.

Powell, Marvin and Bergeron, Jerry. "An Investigation of Differences Between Tenth-, Eleventh-, and Twelfth Grade 'Conforming and Nonconforming' Boys." *The Journal of Educational Research* 56 (December 1962):184-190.

Prows, Mildred J. "An Attempt to Increase Reading Achievement by Organizing Instruction and Sensitizing the Teacher to Build Positive Self-Concepts." *Dissertation Abstracts,* 29, Ann Arbor, Michigan: University Microfilms, a Xerox Company, 1967.

Purkey, William W. *Self-Concept and School Achievement*. Englewood Cliffs, New Jersey: Prentice-Hall, Inc., 1970.

Rogers, Carl R. *Client-Centered Therapy: Its Current Practice, Implications, and Theory*. Boston: Houghton Mifflin Company, 1951.

Rosenthal, Robert, and Jacobson, L. *Pygmalion in the Classroom: Teacher Expectations and Pupils' Intellectual Development*. New York: Holt, Rinehart and Winston, Inc., 1968.

Ruhly, Velma M. "A Study of the Relationship of Self-Concept, Socio-economic Background and Psycholinguistic Abilities to Reading Achievement of Second Grade Males Reading in a Suburban Area." *Dissertation Abstracts*, 31, Ann Arbor, Michigan: University Microfilms, a Xerox Company, 1971.

Russell, David H. "Research on Reading Difficulty and Personality." *Official Report of the American Educational Research Association*, in *Improving Educational Research*. Washington, D.C.: American Educational Research Association, 1948.

Safford, Alton L. "Education of an Individualized Reading Program" *The Reading Teacher* 12 (April 1960):266-270.

Samph, Thomas. "Teacher Behavior and the Reading Performance of Below-Average Achievers." *The Journal of Educational Research* 67 (February 1974):268-270.

Sartain, Harry W. "Individualized Reading: Conclusions Based on Research." In *A Decade of Innovations*, pp. 64-72. Edited by Elaine Vilschek. Newark, Delaware: International Reading Association, 1967.

Savage, R. D. "Personality Factors and Academic Attainment in Junior High School Children." British Journal of Educational Psychology 36 (May 1966):91-92.

Schell, Leo M. An Investigation of Sex Bias in Teacher Assessment of Reading Achievement of Elementary School Pupils. Bethesda, Md.: ERIC Document Reproduction Service, ED 039 118, 1969.

Schroeder, Lily. "A Study of the Relationship Between Five Descriptive Categories of Emotional Disturbance and Reading and Arithmetic Achievement." Exceptional Children 32 (April 1965):11-12.

Schwyhart, Frederick K. "Exploration of the Self-Concept of Retarded Readers in Relation to Reading Achievement." Dissertation Abstracts, 28, Ann Arbor, Michigan: University Microfilms, a Xerox Company, 1967-1968.

Sedarat, Nassir. "Relationship of Achievement Motive, Ego Strength and Certain Aspects of Word Association of the Reading Ability of Intellectually Superior Pupils." Dissertation Abstracts, 28, Ann Arbor, Michigan: University Microfilms, a Xerox Company, 1968.

Seig, Janet. Teacher-Student Congruency and Its Relationship to Reading Achievement. Bethesda, Md.: ERIC Document Reproduction Service, ED 064 698, 1972.

Shapiro, Martin A. "Relationship Among Extroversion, Neuroticism, Academic Reading Achievement and Verbal Learning." Dissertation Abstracts, 28, Ann Arbor, Michigan: University Microfilms, a Xerox Company, 1967-1968.

Silberman, Charles E. Crisis in the Classroom. New York: Random House, 1970.

Singer, Erwin, and Pittman, Marion E. "A Sullivanian Approach to the Problem of Reading Disability: Theoretical Contributions and Empirical Data." Journal of Projective Techniques and Personality Adjustment 24 (September 1965):369-374.

Smith, Nila B. "Research on Reading and Emotions." School and Society 81 (January 1955):8-10.

Southgate, Vera. "The Language Arts in Informal British Primary Classrooms." The Reading Teacher 26 (January 1973):367-373.

Spicola, Rose Frances. "An Investigation into Seven Correlates of Reading Achievement Including Self-Concept." Dissertation Abstracts, 21, Ann Arbor, Michigan: University Microfilms, a Xerox Company, 1961.

Spielberg, Deanna B. "Labeling, Teacher Expectation, Pupil Intelligence Level and Conditions of Learning." Ed.D. dissertation, Boston University, 1973.

Staines, J. W. "The Self-Picture as a Factor in the Classroom." British Journal of Educational Psychology 28 (June 1958):97-111.

Stavrianos, Bertha and Landsman, Sylvia. "Personality Patterns of Deficient Readers with Perceptual-Motor Problems." Psychology in the Schools 6 (April 1969):109-123.

Swartz, Darlene J. The Relationship of Self-Esteem to Reading Performance. Bethesda, Md.: ERIC Document Reproduction Service, ED 006 723, 1972.

Tabarlett, B. E. "Poor Readers and Mental Health." *Elementary English* 35 (December 1958):522-526.

Teigland, Ann E. *An Experimental Study of Individualized and Basal Reader Approaches to Teaching Reading in Grades One and Two.* Bethesda, Md.: ERIC Document Reproduction Service, ED 047 901, 1971.

Thomas, Walter L. *The Thomas Self-Concept Values Test.* Rev. ed. Grand Rapids, Michigan: Educational Service Company, 1969.

Toller, Gladys. "Certain Aspects of the Self-Evaluations by Achieving and Retarded Readers of Average and Above Average Intelligence." *Dissertation Abstracts* 28, Ann Arbor, Michigan: University Microfilms, a Xerox Company, 1967-1968.

Travers, Robert M.W., ed. *Second Handbook of Research on Teaching.* Chicago: Rand McNally and Company, 1973.

Walker, Claire. "An Evaluation of Two Programs in Reading in Grades Four, Five and Six." Ed.D. dissertation, New York University, 1957.

Wallen, Norman E., and Travers, Robert M.W. "Analysis and Investigation of Teaching Methods." In *Handbook of Research on Teaching*, pp. 470-479. Edited by Nathaniel L. Gage. Chicago: Rand McNally and Company, 1963.

Wattenberg, William and Clifford, Clare. "Relations of Self-Concept to Beginning Achievement in Reading." *Child Development* 35 (June 1964):466-467.

Weiner, Roberta. "A Look at Reading Practices in the Open Classroom." *The Reading Teacher* 27 (February 1974): 438-472.

Weintraub, Samuel. "Research: Teacher Expectations and Reading Performance." *The Reading Teacher* 22 (March 1968):555-559

_____; Robinson, H. M.; Smith, H. G.; and Roser. Review of *Reading in Infant Classes*, by E. J. Goodacre. Reading Research Quarterly, 9, No. 3, 1973-1974, pp. 387-388.

Wilkins, William E. *Teacher Expectations and Student Achievement. A Replication Extension, Final Report.* Bethesda, Md.: ERIC Document Reproduction Service,

Williams, Jean H. "The Relationship of Self-Concept and Reading Achievement in First Grade Children." *The Journal of Educational Research* 66 (April 1973): 378-380.

Williams, Robert L., and Cox, Spurgeon. "Self-Concept and School Achievement." *Personnel and Guidance Journal* 46 (January 1968):478-481.

Wood, Joan M. "The Relationship of Self-Concept to Reading Comprehension, Word Meaning and Intelligence." M.Ed. thesis, University of New Hampshire, 1972.

Zimmerman, Irla and Allebrand, George. "Personality Characteristics and Attitudes Toward Achievement." *The Journal of Educational Research* 59 (September 1965): 28-30.

LIBRARY OF DAVIDSON COLLEGE

Books on regular loan may be checked out for two w
be presented at the Circulation D

is cha